To Susan —

DOWNDOG *for* ROADDOGS

With Love

Winifred

DOWNDOG
for
ROADDOGS

*Yoga for Rock-and-Roll Tours
and Other Cosmic Journeys of the Heart*

Winifred Wilson

Copyright © Winifred Wilson, 2021

All rights reserved.
No part of this book may be used or reproduced
in any mannerwhatsoever without written permission
except in the case of brief quotations embodied
in critical articles and reviews.
First printing 2021

ISBN: 978-1-7365914-0-6

Content edited by Robyn Russell
Copy edited by Erin Dvorachek
Photography by Michael Hannig, except page 16
by Paul Shaker and page 183 by Chris Jensen
Book design by Norman Clayton, Ojai, California
Printed in the United States of America

WINIFRED EDITIONS
www.winifredwilson.com

May

all beings

everywhere

be happy

and free.

Contents

Acknowledgements   9

1. Feelin' Alright - *Optimism*   13
2. Dream On - *Vulnerability*   27
3. Love The One You're With - *Purity*   39
4. Shine On You Crazy Diamond - *Strength*   53
5. Landslide - *Surrender*   63
6. Don't Stop Believin' - *Faith*   71
7. While My Guitar Gently Weeps - *Compassion*   83
8. School's Out - *Wonder*   93
9. Tupelo Honey - *Kindness*   105
10. Sunshine Of Your Love - *Gratitude*   117
11. Listen To The Music - *Service*   129
12. Take It Easy - *Ease*   137
13. The Sound Of Silence - *Contentment*   145
14. Can't Find My Way Home - *Authenticity*   157

Endnotes   167
Endorsements   175

Acknowledgements

A wise man once said, "Without help, it is too much for us."
And how true this feels for me.

This book started long before a word was written. Whom I consider my first yoga teacher wasn't a yoga teacher at all in any traditional sense, rather, a professor from my MBA program at Pepperdine University, the divine Dr. Wayne Strom. He taught me to breathe with awareness, and he literally changed my life starting then and there. Working with Wayne charted a course so different than where I was headed, that not only is this a thank you, but a proverbial placing of a wreath of flowers at the feet of my beloved teacher.

It was a mere year later, 2003, that I first stepped onto a yoga mat, which started a journey whereby I've met what feels like my own heart, my tribe, my passion incarnate. Most influential among my teachers are Jimmy Barkan, Kira Sloane, Erich Schiffmann, and Ravi Ravindra, all of whom, in their own way, opened my eyes and lead me further down the path than I could ever go without them. I bow to you all in gratitude.

The writing of this book would not have been possible without my editor and friend, my guide and my soul sister, the brilliant and ever-lovely Robyn Russell.

Thank you to the wise and beautiful Erin Dvorachek whose heart of gold literally touched every letter on these pages. Your standard of excellence made this a better book and made me a better person.

To those friends whose own lives inspire me to go for it, a loving thank you of a thousand suns to Lisa West, Lise Solvang, Roger and Elise Norman, Sally McGrew and Richard Milley, Shep and Katie Gordon, Mick Fleetwood, Lisa Chappel, Franz and Janett Weber, Diane Dunaway, Yvette Thompson, Alice and Sheryl Cooper, Kitty McKay and John Procaccini, Kevin Kohler, Steve and Angie Edelson, Marshall and Paige Stevenson, Melanie Wicker, Danny and

Leslie Zelisko, Pat and Cris Simmons, Lisa Genova, Michael Bolton, Jackie Smaga, Carl and Kim Staub, Melissa Cavanaugh, Gail Swanson, Gail Defferari, Bob Fondiller, Lillian Salerno, Malcolm and Kelley McDowell, Paul Shaker, John and Marcy McFee, Rick Bartolf and Paul Brown, Keith Dehnert, Jim and Rosie Farmer, Bernard Lackner, Kosta and Julie Arger, Jacqui Burge, Cinderella Dietrich, Mark Ellman, Gerry Ellman, Ross and Mary Valory, Amber Williams, Deni Roman, Beth McInerney, Mo'o Tatau and Monique Williams, Kelly Van Unen, Mieko Arakawa, Alan and Sara Schroepfer, Tiffany Carole, and Elise whom is between last names.

To my brothers Walton and Sloan, my Mom Edna, the ever-present spirit of my father Carl, and my aunts and uncles, Miles and Carolyn, and Louis and Lynne. I'm forever grateful to have landed in this nest of family love.

To the wonderful Norman Clayton who brought this book to life by illuminating my manuscript with his tenderness and extraordinary design skills.

To the Dave Mason Band: Johnne, Alvino, Rick, Chris, David G and Tony. Thank you for letting me tag along with you on tour. Deep gratitude to you for sharing all those laughs backstage and your beautiful friendship over the many, many miles.

To my husband David. For everything.

Thank you.

Optimism

Tadasana
Mountain Pose

1
Feelin' Alright

To say I had a midlife crisis wouldn't be entirely accurate—I'd been in a steady and relentless spiritual dilemma for so long that there was nothing midlife about it. The fact that I was 42 seemed overdue, even incidental.

Aadil Palkhivala—a name I would come to know in the following years—said, "The practice of yoga isn't about the shape of a pose, it's about the shape of your life." I didn't walk into my first yoga class with this in mind. Besides, my life was excellent as it was, thank you very much. I was, however, intent on changing the shape of my body, and dreamed of sculpting it into a form so flawless it would rival Barbie's—a role model as unrealistic as the doll is out of date. The notion that "the body is the temple of the spirit" was utter nonsense to me. Appearances were everything.

Self-improvement governed my life then, only it wasn't my real self I was keen on perfecting. Hair extensions, designer clothes, increasingly higher-paying jobs, a luxe car, and a beautiful home were a huge, all-consuming part of this.

When I walked into that first yoga class, all those trappings were not enough. The straightjacket of *should* and *if only* confined me so much my breath had become round-the-clock-shallow. This was likely exacerbated by the enormous saline breasts resting on top of my lungs and squeezing the carefully-orchestrated life right out of me. Pranayama was torturous; each breath struggled to push away the heaviness of a body fraught with fear and humiliation. I wasn't breathing much at all, really, but gasping for air, striving for the very thing so freely given to us.

I didn't realize how suffocating all my pretense was until that initial attempt at the 5,000-year-old practice. It was a bleak January day, dry and cold outside, warm and inviting inside—not only in terms of a thermostat set to a balmy 75, but also with the bevy of perky yogis at the sign-in desk. I didn't trust their enthusiasm, but I proceeded anyway, albeit with caution, the way I usually moved through the world. I didn't have much faith in anything then, but I also didn't have a whole lot to lose, which is another way of saying I was desperate. I wasn't just panicky during that time, either—I was borderline frantic. Nothing felt safe; nothing felt nourishing. I'd never admit these things to myself so I'd just blame all my problems on those "last five pounds" I needed to lose. So, armed with a rubber mat and a bottle of water, I strode through a door labeled "Quiet Zone." The formal practice area hovered over 100 degrees. I sat down on my mat, looked around nervously, and fidgeted with my yoga clothes, trying to look like anything but a beginner.

Within the first three minutes, the warm and fuzzy feel of the studio turned inferno-like. I'm convinced this was due to the anger and self-hatred that seared inside of me as I was forced to watch my reflection in the wall of mirrors at the front of the room. Sweat rolled off my body as I began to move, while the other students—seemingly blissfully, definitely determined—breathed and warrior-ed and perspired around me.

But soaking my mat wasn't so much sweat—it was tears. No matter that I'd spent most of my adolescence and adulthood sizing myself in front of a mirror: Up until that point I'd never really seen myself. I'd spent years plastering my face with makeup and cloaking my body in clothes, but had never paused long enough to see the woman inside. Some inescapable truth stared back at me in that hot-as-hell yoga class. *You are insecure*, my reflection seemed to say. *You lack. And you have shame.* Decades of sorrow, I realized, had been held back by sheer, stout pride.

Illusions I'd entertained about myself disintegrated right along with those tears that fell on my sky-blue, brand-new yoga mat. I tried to conceal what I perceived as weak and embarrassing from the other students, just like I was doing out in the world. The money I'd spent to beautify myself, the energy I'd put forth to have a life I wasn't sure was mine, the body I'd hated and mistreated, the fake happiness and stuffed regrets, guilt, and dread—all came into hyper-real focus as I stood in the realization that I wasn't close to the person I wanted to be, the person I knew I could be, and the deep, unadorned self that was screaming out to just *be*.

That's precisely when the yoga teacher instructed us to gather on the top of our mats and stand still in tadasana, or mountain pose. To just stand there seemed so simple—so ridiculously easy—that it struck me as absurd. This was what yoga was about—standing at the top of your mat with your feet spread hips-width apart? I wanted my money back.

And yet, within the span of a few breaths, I realized that tadasana is a deceptively challenging pose. It asks practitioners to be firm and quiet on their feet. It asks practitioners to *stand* on their own two feet, and feel their strength and hope rise out of the crowns of their heads.

It was awful and revolutionary at once. I freaked as I faced myself head-on in the mirrors in front of me. (I see, now, why it's called a looking glass.) I encountered a watered down, de-glamourized version of myself in plain and absolute view. I wanted to run and I wanted to crumble but I held my ground. For once, I didn't act upon my inclination to flee. What was this thing called yoga?

The great Christopher Reeve said, "True transformation takes either courage or disaster." For me it was a mix of both, and in the months after I assumed my first tadasana my life fell apart and came together all at once.

I started going to class every day. It was the only place I felt I could stand still and breathe while my world around me went to pieces. I left my husband of fifteen years, my long career in the art gallery business, my beloved house, my dog—everything that kept my life shiny and tidy—and headed to California. Not in a bold and empowered way, mind you. One day I just picked up and left, which is a kinder way to say that I gave up. Too chicken for suicide, I opted to be rescued by a man I barely knew. I jumped in my 500SL Mercedes Benz with a suitcase and some cash and raced down the freeway, driving as fast as I could to get away from myself and towards him. It felt urgent and necessary, these leaps I was making, but

Yoga

is breaking the

bonds

of suffering.

〰 *Bhagavad Gita* 6:23

in truth I was unsure, neurotic, and more than a little terrified. My new yoga practice had unhinged me.

Turns out this state of mind is the worst way to start a new life, like, ever. In no time flat, I was striving to stand on my own two feet in the studio of life. I was also searching for something, *anything*, Out There that would make me feel better. Compassion, honesty, and accountability would have been better travel companions than Gucci and chardonnay, but I wasn't open to deep change. I basically wanted to stay the same inside, just shift my outside. You know: Better man, cooler outfits, cuter yoga studios, a superior zip code. The usual suspects.

I landed in Ojai, California, for an overnight visit. Within a month, the Southern California enclave became my home, as much as for the yoga community I found as for the man I'd come to see. Seemed like everybody was doing yoga there; spiritual living was practically trendy. And while I didn't have the slightest idea what people were talking about when Ram Dass entered the conversation, I reveled in the fact I that didn't see a single designer handbag in the entire town. Nobody drove fancy cars.

My first real friend in that town was the deity Ganesha, known as the remover of obstacles. He appealed to me because I thought if I chanted enough he'd step in and do the hard work of transformation for me. I bought a sparkly gemstone Ganesha necklace in his honor and wore it to show how spiritually serious I was. It was to no avail: In those first bewildering months, my life got worse—way worse—and I was left standing still alright, but also broke and alone and addicted.

Decades earlier, Rock-and-Roll Hall-of-Famer Dave Mason penned "Feelin' Alright" with a question mark after the title. He also underlined the next sentence "not feelin' too good myself." A few years after the song's debut on a Traffic album, Joe Cocker got ahold of it and turned it into the upbeat mantra we now know as "Feelin' Alright!" I've always loved the questioning in Dave's original draft but I also admire how that exclamation mark—and a little Cocker magic—completely changed that song.

Yoga, I discovered, is like that too. It presents you with the material but it's up to you to work with it. Interpretation can change a song and it will damn well change your life. One definition from the *Bhagavad Gita* claims the practice is "the breaking of the bonds of suffering." As I came to learn, yoga promotes perspective, a new way of seeing. Only it isn't a look outside at all. It's a profound peering in.

There is nothing sweet and easy about this. Yoga doesn't sugarcoat, ignore, or numb negative feelings, just as yogis are not unaware that life is defined by difficulties—even Buddha's first noble truth is "Life is Suffering." Rather, yoga points out that it's the dwelling in our misery, the clinging to our tight spots, that fuels our unease. Yoga shifts the spotlight on our interior terrain not to remove ourselves from the world but to be in her with greater integrity, authenticity, and heart. It requires radical responsibility for our life, which might account for why the life of a yogi isn't necessarily easy. There is nothing outside to blame.

I didn't come to these lessons overnight. I was, after all, a girl who prioritized how I looked. My "bonds of suffering" were thick and sticky (and expensive) things. I hung onto my Ganesha necklace with both hands as I waited for those ties to start dissolving and happiness to arrive, that spiritual crisis still simmering. Headlines from glossy magazine covers and promises from blissful yoga teachers weren't happening for me. I wasn't feeling better or more peaceful or purer; in fact, I'd never been so undone. All my brilliant thinking and mega-efforts to look like Malibu Barbie were for naught under yoga's candid glare. It got so bad (or good, depending on where we are in the story) that I landed in an alcohol treatment center. Which, really, is one big-ass, long tadasana pose.

Tadasana holds you upright in stillness so you can get a higher perspective. She's one of those poses that's easy to take for granted, like life itself. People—me included—may ask, what's the big deal, to just stand there? I say, now, that it is everything. It's being fully present—not mired in the past, or soaring into the future. It's awareness of where you are, today, in this minute. The first yoga sutra says *atha yoga anushasanam*: "the teaching of yoga is here and now," because the here and now is all we really have, and the only place we can begin to make any real change is directly before us. Or, rather, inside of us.

The realities I encountered in getting sober were stern and unyielding. Sure, the treatment center was a container that held me steady and mountain-like during massive inner turbulence, and Sir Edmund Hilary may have said that "it's not the mountains we conquer, but ourselves." So what? I would rather have tried to scale Mt. Everest than confront myself. What I also didn't know is that rock bottom will teach you lessons that mountaintops never will. But Hilary's dictum was a fitting metaphor, and one I latched onto as I tried to imagine navigating life without a man beside me and a wine glass in my hand.

In the ancient yoga texts and beyond, mountains are among the most important symbols of enlightened daily living, of overcoming hindrances, of finding strength and loftier endeavors. And while mountain pose is the essence of foundation and stability—the number one pose of all standing poses—there is equal energy in the rising she requires. Even as our feet are grounded, our inner arches are lifting. The elevation of our spine, meanwhile, allows proper placement of the head, which then aligns with the heart. There is a sense of drawing up as a grander power beckons, away from earthbound attachments. It all seemed so splendid to me—so promising—as I sweated out 20 years of booze and bad decisions and delved into the 12-step process.

Jetsunma Tenzin Palmo describes a yogini as "a professional of the interior landscape."

After my 45 days in rehab I changed career tracks for this more nebulous pursuit. I ditched three decades of executive work and did the only thing I wanted to do: I started teaching yoga. My family worried about me; my friends thought I'd lost my mind. And perhaps I had, which wasn't altogether a bad thing—my "unguarded thoughts," as Buddha calls them, were causing more harm than anything else. Breaking my addiction to white wine and Versace slingbacks was one matter; changing my attitude towards life was quite another. Sticking close to the yoga practices seemed like a wise place to park for a while.

After rehab I resumed living in Ojai, the place I'd run to in search of love, misguided as it was. The Topatopa Mountains above the city run east to west, which allows the sun to rise at one end of the valley and set at the other, supplying some of the longest, most spectacular sunrises and sunsets in the world. In those first months of sobriety, when everything was tender and raw and new, and all of my feelings—from shame to resentment—could no longer be subdued by Viognier and Betsey Johnson, the journey of the sun seemed wildly symbolic of consciousness's ever-changing light. Just as the sun would disappear, the mountains would turn whisper-pink, my favorite color, hinting that even the impending dark was bound to be beautiful. How crazy it seemed then—that I could love myself despite my soul's proverbial nights. Yogis claim the path of healing involves seeing ourselves clearly, including our shadow side. Long time Ojai Valley resident and sage Krishnamurti said, "If you see what is, what is changes." I spent the better part of a decade doing my best to look.

But it wasn't until I really grasped that tadasana isn't a static posture that the pose came alive for me. Another name commonly used for it is *samasthiti*. Translated as "equal standing," it evokes a command to attention; to stand in balanced immobility in an attempt to bring an evenness to the right and the left, the front and the back, the light and the dark. It leaves nothing out.

After a decade of teaching and practicing yoga—of finally finding comfort in standing still—I was knocked off-balance when the love interest I'd chased ten years earlier asked me to join the tour life with him. His name? Dave Mason.

Yes, the very hand that penned "Feelin' Alright" also picked up mine and helped lift me from the dredges. The very person I thought would be my magic carpet ride to all things sex, drugs, and rock-and-roll turned out to be one of the most influential people on my path to sobriety. He'd stayed by my side all those years, strong and steady, hilarious and complex, as I unwound old patterns and explored healthier versions of self.

Here,

now,

is the teaching

of yoga.

◆ The Yoga Sutras of Patanjali
Sutra 1.1 (trans. Ravi Ravindra)

His steadfastness was and is no wonder: The man is a veritable powerhouse. Dave has played with some of the most remarkable musicians of our time; George Harrison, Jimi Hendrix, the Rolling Stones, Michael Jackson, and Fleetwood Mac are just a few among them. He also doesn't stop, and has been performing, continually, for 50 years.

But, while Dave may have written some of the greatest love songs I've ever heard, we all know that domestic responsibilities and quotidian tensions strain a relationship. His heavy tour schedule offered space and safe distance. It's how I liked it.

I was obstinate as ever towards his suggestion. A decade of yoga out the door in a single ask. I didn't want to change—not again, and not for a man *again*. I was content where I was. My well-worn Ganesha necklace had at long last taken on real meaning. There wasn't a chance I'd give up my hard-won independence and stability to join my partner for a life on the road.

And yet, that's the thing about tadasana: Once you get the hang of it, you can move on to more sophisticated and challenging postures. If yoga means union and I barely saw Dave long enough to really cultivate a connection, what kind of yogi was I?

For the record, Dave Mason doesn't let many people in. He comes across as tough and seemingly uncaring but that's actually not the case at all. He's the opposite, and what's misunderstood as gruff is the grit of a lifetime of artistic living. He's had his heart broken more than anyone I've ever known, yet if there's anything I've learned it's that the heart doesn't stretch in only one direction.

David, his birth name, and the name those close to him use, is cuddlier and more casual than his celebrity persona. Dave is the assumed name for the performer, the act, the image that he's built through his nonstop shows. David's love of music is as real as it comes. It's his first love—it's his main love—and so when he asked me to join him on tour, and not in a weekend-once-in-a-while schedule, but over 100 shows over the course of a year, I was stunned. Then I was resistant. And then I dove in.

I left my job as a yoga teacher to join him on tour, but quickly discovered that yoga is something you never really leave. While rolling across the continental U.S. in a confined, chaotic space, I became a student again and started assessing the reliability of yogic theories and practices—which, believe me, look a lot different on a tour bus in the parking lot of a Hampton Inn during an East Coast winter after your third 12-hour working day than in a clean, brightly-lit studio on California's affluent coast.

  Like my first tadasana, I was frustrated and wanted to quit right away, mainly because I wasn't very good at it. There was plenty of "not feeling too good myself." Touring felt disorienting and ungrounding; it was, really, the antithesis of the yoga I'd come to know. It stole my sleep, my privacy, and all my clean clothes. Organic greens became a distant memory. I was tirelessly reminded that my dance had no rhythm, I couldn't carry a tune and was an outsider in every way. I wanted out, and fast.

  Then, late one night backstage, with "All Along The Watchtower" in full roar, I stood watching the show and realized that I was almost in tadasana. A knee-high leather boots and sequin jacket almost-tadasana. Only the pose was…off. No matter how cute my outfit was, inside I was brimming with fury and despair, feeling victimized by external difficulties, which frankly amounted to working a lot harder than I thought I'd have to on the road and manning the merch table and in a relationship with a musician. Tadasana is one of those poses that takes effort to align, just like joy and gratitude, and I'd chosen gloom and doom. I couldn't see the amazing show in front of me because I was blinded by homesickness and the eternal delusion that the grass is always greener on the other side.

  When insight struck, she was still and quiet. This was miraculous enough in the middle of a rock show, but the real magic was the realization that it *does* count how you take a stand and hold your heart, no matter what's going on around you. Later, throughout the years of touring with David—of, literally, letting the rubber meet the road—what seems to matter the most, whether I'm in an ashram in India or in a cold concert hall basement in Albany, is, where is my heart? Where is my attention?

I paused where I was during that show. I stood straighter, and put the toes of my boots together, my heels slightly apart. I firmed my thigh muscles and tightened my kneecaps. Then I widened my collarbones and lifted my sternum straight up to the sky and said, *hello, world.* I am here. And I am listening.

Touring stretches me day in, day out. It takes me out of my safe haven and exposes my limits. I crave the security and familiarity of my home, sure, but the gift here has been in learning how to take refuge in connecting with life and standing still and contained throughout it all.

The myths say Shiva—the god of transformation—lives in the mountains, but in practice he lives in our hearts. Shiva is also known as Aniketa, which translates to "without a home." This book isn't a call to be homeless, of course, or to leave home to go on a rock-and-roll tour in search of transformation. While the book chronicles my experience on the unlikely seats of a rock-and-roll tour bus, the "ride" I was on is mere allegory for the ever-changing, often-loud, and frantically-paced era in which we now live. What you're holding here is an invitation to be present in our own hearts, so that we are at home in the world and with each other, anyplace, anytime.

The Sanskrit word *asana* usually translates to "seat" and brings to mind the physical practices, like tadasana, that are required for meditation. But *asana* also holds the deeper meaning *attitude.* The sutras suggest, "When presented with disquieting thoughts or feelings, cultivate an opposite, elevated attitude."

It's nurturing feelin' alright, instead of "not feelin' too good myself." The song lyrics are always there. But, as you'll see in the pages that follow, it's a matter of how you sing them.

Vulnerability

Utkatasana Hybrid
Curtsy Pose

2
Dream On

I feel vulnerable just wearing white after Labor Day. Meaning, never in a million years did I set out to be in music or in a band, let alone on a rock-and-roll tour that would traverse the country and hit up venues in almost every one of the fifty states. I've never had the confidence to be seen in such a big way, all those eyes on me night after night, watching my every move and casting opinions. (We all act like we aren't judgmental but we are.) Touring is, to be sure, a formidable form of exposure.

Vulnerability is painful because, paradoxically, openness often feels like disconnection. Moreover, letting go of behaviors that promote surefire acceptance feels risky as hell. To make myself feel safe and loved I've long constructed walls, confining myself behind the barricades of being a nice girl—a go-with-the-flow kind of gal—even if it meant I had to abandon the more real parts of me, the ones that asked to be heard, and keep my own hopes and dreams out of sight and away from assessment. Getting sober and practicing yoga have helped with vulnerability, yes, but 50 years of people-pleasing and codependency don't evaporate overnight.

Remaining closed-off and protected was relatively easy to manage in the first eight years of my relationship with David. We lived together but led separate lives. Our house was perched atop a hill on the east end of Ojai, where, together, we loved to sit outside to enjoy the gorgeous view of the valley. At least we did when he was in town, which was only a few days a month, most months. In addition to teaching yoga during those years, I was also building a nonprofit and working with women recovering from substance abuse. David was, of course, touring. Our dual careers were our lifelines, while our time together was short, sweet, and sexy. It was almost as handy and uncomplicated as being married to an astronaut. Long distance love is blissful and easy because it gives you a lot of space to hide. It's tidy and succinct, which is how I like things anyway.

Part of the reason I joined David on the road was to learn more yoga—which may seem ironic, considering that I left teaching yoga to do so. But yoga, from the Sanskrit word *yuj*, or "to yoke," means connection, and it's a hard thing to find with your spouse when you have two different lives and live in two different places. Much to my dismay, because it seemed to work for a good, long while. Spending time together between tours felt like mini-vacations, where it was easy to hang in the surface; brevity, after all, lets you put forth your best self. You only have to be fabulous for short spurts of time.

Somehow through all this long distance David and I fell in love, really in love. This was in spite of ourselves. They say it happens like that sometimes, that love appears when you stop looking so hard. For me it happened when I quit trying to be so damn loveable. I lost the fake hair, fake fingernails, and fake boobs, got sober and got genuine. I didn't know who Dave Mason was when I met him, and we both had to drop our usual tactics that held us guarded, untouchable, and entirely unsuitable for meaningful, intimate relationships.

Going on tour with him was a daunting prospect for many reasons, some mundane and some material, but what was most terrifying of all was that I would be seen. I'd be deeply exposed in a subculture I knew so little about I couldn't even fake being cool because I didn't know what the protocol was in the first place. It wasn't as simple as "leaving my comfort zone," as described by all those self-help books on my overstuffed shelf, because there was no such zone. I was crazy intimidated by the standard of devotion to music I'd been witnessing in David from afar, and to be close to it 24/7 would shine a spotlight on the holes in my own dreams and passions. I was also highly uncomfortable around David's band family (the musicians and crew), his team of accountants, talent bookers, marketing and PR professionals; and by his legions of fans, most of whom had been following him a lot longer than I had even heard of him. I belonged with him—of this I was sure. What I wasn't so sure about was if I belonged in the world he rolled in.

But the most frightening gamble of all was being seen by David. With him, my life felt the most enthused but also the most fragile. A willingness to be seen and to love with your whole heart—even though there exists the possibility that you might not get loved back for showing your flaws—struck me as a way bigger risk than stepping on stage because, well, it's completely personal. *You are the music.* Overall, I was venturing into new territory on all fronts, no cities or oceans or even walls between us. Heck, we would barely have doors. Not only would we be living together, but we would also be working and traveling side by side, in a 45 x 8 foot Prevost bus, which looks a lot bigger than it actually feels once you're inside.

It's a handsome and tasteful space, thank goodness, with dark, cherry wood paneling, granite countertops, and Salvador Dali etchings throughout. The front area, behind the driver's seat, is a "common area" complete with captain's chairs, a dining table, a galley kitchen, and a designer bathroom. The back third of the bus is the bedroom and a second bathroom. Sandwiched between the two is no man's land, but since we'd converted the bunk space into a closet on one side and a "laundry room" on the other, there was and is nowhere to run for cover. I mean, really, how can a girl be awesome *all of the time?*

Now, we're in the same space day in and day out, which, in the absence of walls, feels more like mirrors. The yogis say we can't see in others what we can't see in ourselves, and when your habitual tendency is to be outrageously hard on yourself, you can understand that this was no joy ride. *Is he really going to wear that stained t-shirt with a rip...again? Did he used to chew this loudly? Did I; do I?*

The intensity in the front of the bus—or, more accurately, in my mind—sent me dive-bombing regularly behind the halfway mark between the "public" seating area and kitchen and the "private" office/bedroom. The door here is usually open while driving, because even though it's a big bus, it's a bus, and to state the obvious, the more open, the better. It gives the illusion of space.

But me, I shut the door. With a single press of a button, a sliding wood panel door created a barrier. The gentle thud as it locked into place always prompted an audible sigh of relief.

I did a lot of hanging out behind this door on that first tour. As we rolled along the interstate, I grew more and more frustrated staring at it too. I longed for my daily yoga practice; For fresh air, acai bowls, and wide, open spaces. There was calm and order in my pre-tour days: An early bedtime, a lot of kale salad, good friends. It was defined by stability and repetition, and I knew precisely what was expected of me: Show up early for class, prepare the space, teach class, close the studio. Repeat.

I didn't know what I was supposed to do on tour. Or, rather, who I was supposed to be. Wife? Merch girl? Band buddy? Bus maid? VIP coordinator? Tour hostess? Dog walker? Chef? *Groupie?* Some combination of all of the above? None of the above? It was all so confusing—it all left me so shaky—I began to see why, in the *Bhagavad Gita*, Arjuna the Warrior commences his spiritual learning from a state of bewilderment.

To combat despondency and disorientation, I found ground in the only thing available: My body. I picked up my practice of yoga anew in the tiny hallway between the laundry room and the closet, which, measuring 4 ft across and 6 ft long, turned out to be all I needed for my Manduka travel mat. There was just enough room to do forward-facing poses—like warriors—as well as the splits and some compact seated postures. I committed to all of this as we drove everywhere from Denver to Dallas, while also adjusting to life with a man who wasn't on the moon but two feet away from me. In other words, very *un*steady ground.

There, I realized something obvious, but vital: The first step towards being real and living your dreams often comes down to stop hating where are you are so much. "There is no happiness in any place," writes Henry David Thoreau, "except what you bring to it yourself." Sages from all traditions tell us happiness and contentment starts and ends inside. It was—also obvious, also necessary—about doing more of what you love; of answering those calls that reside deep within your heart.

For me, that's yoga. But my two little Maltese dogs—Lucy and

Star—ran around my feet, making it even trickier to practice. I was irritated and confused. Couldn't I at least make *yoga* work? Arjuna was on a battlefield in his bafflement because he didn't know how to fight. I'd been teaching yoga for fifteen years and didn't know how to practice. Finally, I asked myself, what does sticking to pre-prescribed formalities do for you anyway in this narrow hall? It didn't look like yoga but it felt like it. Yoga began coming through, and at last dropped from my head to my heart.

I also began to see why Buddhist meditators practice facing walls. It directs you back toward yourself, and as Brene Brown says, "Our sense of belonging can never be greater than our level of self-acceptance." There is no escaping vulnerability except by looking honestly within. There's also no growth without it. The melting of our self-judgment is the only way to soothe feeling separate from everybody else. Plus, it's good to be reminded that the fear of confronting parts of ourselves is far scarier than facing another's.

Realization happens during profound moments, or when you're staring at your abdomen upside down while going 70mph—instances that stop us in our customary habits of seeing and hearing. Trying to do *asana* in a tiny, moving space completely blew down my walled-in, small thinking of what yoga should look like. Realizations of many sorts invite vulnerability because it acknowledges and exposes shortcomings and discontent. But it boomerangs in the opposite direction too, and sends the mind to Pluto by considering all of the possibilities around and within us. *Dream on*, people say with snarkiness nowadays, but I prefer Aerosmith's fervent instruction instead.

Besides, how do we define space, really? On tour, with very little privacy, an area that holds nothing more than my mat is practically palatial. The more and more I wiggled around to find space on it, the more and more essential it became to start touring inward. As I stepped on my mat, the movement around and below me became centered, so much so I could tune in to the present moment. "Sing with me, just for today," Aersosmith bellows, which reminded me, literally, to take it *one day at a time*—advice that was as potent in the first days of touring as it was in my early years of sobriety. And, like I found in sobriety, I felt new muscles firing and new possibilities of doing old things in new ways. Right there crossing the highway I reached a crossroad... of facing the unfamiliar versus the safety and comfort of all that I had come to trust. I became my own rolling yoga tour.

Steven Tyler says that "Dream On" is "about the hunger to be somebody; Dream until your dreams come true." Dreaming is different than fantasy; it suggests the possibility that you *can* change your life. Dreaming holds the whisper of belief that you possess the goods and are willing to do the work to forge a new path. The biggest adventure of this tour life was happening in a confined hallway, and the trip was an internal one.

Dreaming drove me to start living life in radical amazement. This may sound high-falutin, but once you start opening your eyes to the world, there's suddenly awe all around you. I was amazed that I could live without doing a proper Sun A and still stay flexible. That I could quiet my mind without once chanting OM. That the security guard in Hartford who didn't "practice yoga" was intuitive enough to bring me a chair so I didn't have to stand all night at merch. That the sunrise in Chester, New Jersey can take your breath away every bit as a sunset in Makena, Maui. That everywhere we went, without exception, I found kind people. That it really doesn't matter if your fingernail polish is chipped. That the Hampton Inn actually does make pretty good waffles. That David is not just funny, he's hilarious. That the willingness to show up and be seen can deliver countless gifts.

"Vulnerability is the birthplace of creativity," Brene says, and I believe this is true because my yoga practice completely changed on a bus cruising through Somewhere, USA from a girl who wanted to be Anywhere Else But There. First, I had to get through the questions that arrive with any sort of vulnerability: Could I really continue to practice yoga in an atmosphere and a culture decidedly unyoga? On a *rock-and-roll tour*? Amidst a selection of snacks where salt and vinegar potato chips were considered a delicacy? In the throes of merch madness where a guest held up the line while he told me his whole life story in explicit detail, including his "spiritual" experience of dropping acid at his first Dave concert? I wanted to not only maintain the practice of loveliness promoted by yoga, but to thrive in it. I wanted to break boundaries, get stronger, deepen my study of the poses, learn more Sanskrit, snuggle up to the texts—all of which I'd have plenty of time to do once I quit sulking, slinking behind walls, and crying in my Chai tea, which, to be fair, coming out of a mass market box tasted like dirt compared to Ojai's Farmer and the Cook's handmade blend.

"You got to lose to know how to win," Tyler says, and my worry is he's right. I'd lost my life as a yoga teacher and designer Chai drinker in California but I was just beginning my adventure as a yogi in the larger world, which, ironically, was also in a much, *much* smaller space. While the band was singing on stage I was singing "for the laughter, sing(ing) for the tears" and seeking refuge on my mat—no longer as a place to hide, but as a place to create. And given the itty-bitty space I had to work in, I had no choice but to innovate *something else*.

It was there that I made some poses up, like the curtsy. It's not one you'll find in classic yoga books. It's not really standing or sitting. The beauty of it is that it's both centered and asymmetrical—part dance, part static—and, like ukatasana, or chair pose, you can transition from it to almost any other posture. It's a gesture of greeting, and like all greetings it summons a smooth transition from vulnerability to being seen.

The measurements of my rolling yoga studio may have inspired the pose but it's derived from my Texan youth. The "Texas Dip" is an extreme curtsy performed by a debutante. The young woman holds her arms out to the side, then slowly lowers her forehead towards the floor by crossing her ankles, bending her knees, and sinking. When the debutante's head nears the floor, she turns her head sideways, averting the catastrophe of getting lipstick on her gown. This move is exceedingly difficult, especially when wearing high heels and under the glaring lights of a stage and the gaze of a room full of people who are there solely to judge you. The curtsy goes back to 1909. It's custom, and proper, and deemed high culture in Texas.

As a native Texan you might say this pose is in my blood. We were made to curtsy as teenagers at Dick Chaplin's School of Dance, a teenage social dance studio that was more etiquette training than actual dancing. How silly a curtsy seemed at the time, but in retrospect, our social customs were sweet and lovely. We were all on our best behavior at Dick Chaplin's. We were thirteen and there were boys, asking us to dance. We became vulnerable as we lined up single file, our backs to the wall, waiting for a boy to walk from the other side of the room and pick us to be his partner. Just standing there, our little hearts wide open, our hair all washed and curled, in our pretty, fresh, formal dresses and little white gloves. And we curtseyed.

I found it funny that it resurfaced thirty-plus years later on a rock-and-roll tour when not once, it's safe to say, did I worry about getting lipstick on a fancy formal gown. Perhaps the desire to create this pose was a lurking call to the feminine in me to rise; a way to access the feeling of a puffy dress and long white gloves; a means to feel pretty and graceful amidst the grunge of the road; a method to feel fresh, inspired, and young again. Whatever the case may be, it worked.

Those days of dance lessons seem so far away. The curtsy, however, remains close. I no longer take it for granted; rather, I'm grateful my knees and ankles can bend me into the pose at my age. And the Texas Dip? I can barely get up from that position, much less with poise and a bouquet of flowers in one hand. But part of what's vulnerable and brave is seeing myself in this pose at the age of 58. I mean, I've never seen so many lines on my face until I started touring (but I've also never had the guts to really look, either—walls help you do that when you hit them). "Every time when I look in the mirror, All these lines on my face getting clearer," Tyler sings, and I'm pretty sure he's talking to me, or at least anyone who's been on the road. The dirt, the late hours, the processed food, the forced air, the ever-changing, sometimes dramatic climate changes—it all takes a toll on one's face. No perfect debutante skin could survive a single season out here. No proper high society woman would be caught dead on a tour. But these wrinkles are all part of the "dues in life to pay;" these curveballs thrown by the Divine that demand we take a path completely unplanned. It's so worth the price of wisdom, the opportunity to experience things differently and in ways never planned, which has allowed me to see that the curtsy pose is also a bow of gratitude. Brene Brown says, "what makes you vulnerable, makes you beautiful," and nothing shines brighter than one who is living a bold, inspired life. (Although a jar of good face cream helps.)

Life can be tremendously hard at times—especially when our vulnerabilities are exposed to ourselves and others, and particularly when we're tested—but these are moments of our greatest learning because they're the times, the yogis would say, of our greatest blindness. I'm not sure I would have seen these depths from the shelter of a proper studio. Touring has made the practice of vulnerability alive and exhilarating. It feels as fresh as the first time I curtsied in front of Steve Thomas at Dick Chaplin's. It was the first time I danced with a boy, and not just any boy—I had a huge crush on this guy. He was a football player and a basketball player and had the most gorgeous, beach-curled hair I'd ever seen. My curtsy meant I'd have to present myself and then leave the information I found in his beautiful blue eyes in order to bow my head for a short, very precarious moment. "The strongest love is love that demonstrates fragility," writes Paulo Coelho. This leads me to think that vulnerability is actually tour medicine. My relationship with David will never be the same. My yoga practice is forever changed. My path in this world is taking on a new meaning where dreams are no longer the realm of whimsy or something *other people do.*

The *Bhagavad Gita* says, "The wise man lets go of all results, whether good or bad, and is focused on the action alone. Yoga is skill in action." The temptation is thinking we can coerce the universe to use our actions to our benefit. It's like doing a load of David's laundry to manipulate him to stop for a sightseeing adventure.

Which never works. So finally I've learned to do the laundry simply because it needs to get done. While I'm practicing yoga as a way to learn how to teach, I'm also practicing because, like the laundry, it needs doing. It keeps me sane in a tour world that is anything but ordered. It keeps me inspired to stay vulnerable and dream big, none of which can happen if I'm hiding behind that sliding wall, refusing to open the door.

Purity

Ustrasana
Camel Pose

3

Love The One You're With

Yoga isn't about the state of your pose—it's about the state of your heart. This is the action that's truly critical, which is why the *Bhagavad Gita* talks more about the qualities of a yogi than the deeds of one. If the actor is right, then her actions are correct. It's not so much what you're doing as *how you are doing it*. The best yoga teachers know that it isn't the perfection of a posture that matters—it's our willingness to attempt it. This distinction is essential. There's a general temptation to get caught up in examining our actions, but not in examining ourselves, and endeavoring any pose—or any life change—asks us to do the latter first if anything is to be accomplished.

The practices of yoga help cleanse our opinions and declutter our hearts. It's intimate and personal and sometimes painful, because with awareness of any kind comes responsibility. It's up to us and us alone to make any real change in our behavior and, thus, our lives.

While it seems that I changed my life by jumping on a rock-tour bus, not much changed at first, at least not internally, where it matters the most. "Wherever you go, there you are," Jon Kabat-Zinn said. I never quite believed this, not really, until I toured. I was running and running, and my shadow kept following me. It made it hard to sit still.

Tucked onto the second rung of yoga's eight limb path is the suggestion of *saucha*, which is typically translated as "cleanliness." As the first of the five *niyamas*—or personal observances—it asks practitioners to maintain a clean mind, body, nature, and even manner of speech.

This is important, sure, but it seems secondary to the requirements of tour life, where being on time, showing up at the right place, and knowing the set list are far more pressing issues than being freshly showered and having good breath. A *real* rock-and-roll show never promises either of these things, anyway.

As a yogi, I've always breezed right over *saucha*. I checked off its box with a *yes, obvz, got it*; I've been well-coiffed since I was six. I knew how to match the ribbon in my hair to my dress before I knew how to do subtraction, treated my teeth with as much dedication and care as an orthodontist's daughter, and spent an inordinate amount of time in my mother's powder room, sampling her soaps and potions and lotions.

This, however, isn't *saucha*—not really, anyway. It's more than a matter of matchy-match clothes and staying freshly bathed and clothed, or of keeping your house tidy. The sutras are short aphorisms. They extend to every level—physical, mental, spiritual. Patanjali declares that *saucha* brings about pleasantness, which seems obvious to me until you've polished yourself into believing the state of your outfit and the spotlessness of your house determines your worth.

Saucha is a spiritual law, which renders it much harder to do in the subtle, internal realms. It implies a heart free from unloving thoughts; a mind and spirit unpolluted by negativity. Rumi says, "Your task is not to seek for love, but merely to seek and find all the barriers within yourself that you have built against it." The practice of *saucha* is cleansing the perceptions that hold us back from realizing this. Tour life, however, moves so fast it's difficult to find time for a shower, let alone the space to scrub your thoughts clean so you can see love all around you.

But joining a man who has been touring for 50 years—and living in close quarters with him—demands finding time for both. During that first tour, I took it upon myself to be the shiny and neat one, pleasant to look at and a breeze to live with. I felt like it was all on me to learn how to do this new life together—*his* life—and I overcompensated for my massive insecurity by sweeping my surface clean with fresh clothes and clean hair and by stuffing anything unpleasant or ragged out of sight, much like I used to clean my house before the maid service came over. (God forbid someone see a used coffee cup and think I was incapable of order.)

David, meanwhile, is a classic Taurus: reliable, practical, devoted, responsible, stable, a little slovenly. He is also stubborn, impatient, and uncompromising—all necessary skills for thriving in a life lived primarily on the road. (I've seen these inclinations serve him well at home too.) His tenacity is especially potent. He'll work on a song for hours, getting a chord exactly right by staying up all night and wrestling with a single riff. I've seen him take apart a whole "finished" song only to reassemble it with such mastery and precision the piece sounds completely new when it's finished. I know he's done with a song because there'll be something different in his eyes, a relaxed satisfaction of tapped magic, inside. I can also tell he's finished a session because there'll be a sink full of dishes, empty Pellegrino bottles strewn around the studio, and half-smoked cigars in ashtrays. I always clean his studio after he's done, commemorating the creation and artful conclusion of a song in an almost ceremonious manner.

On the Prevost, though, I had a different attitude. His studio was my kitchen, dining room, and den, and I had about as much tolerance for messes in my living space as I did a spot of dirt on my Betsey Johnson baby-doll dress. David didn't even seem to notice it.

"We are most alive when we are in love," John Updike wrote, and David is the most vibrant when he's immersed in Music. He's in his own world a lot of the time, but particularly when he's on tour. I had romantic visions of just the two of us meandering down the highway in a swanky bus, doing dazzling concerts, visiting family and friends everywhere from glittering cities to bucolic farms. There was nothing messy about the version of tour life I constructed—no house to clean, no unpleasant *"us"* to ram into closets and drawers. Just the open road before us during an eternal sunset, my hand warm in his.

The tour itinerary always looks promising at first. We start out organized, well-rested, freshly fed and washed. I felt especially prepared for our first journey together by showing up to that initial tour with an enormous assortment of adorable outfits, like a million too many, enough skincare products to fill the shelves of both bathrooms, sightseeing maps, books to read, and yoga paraphernalia so extensive I could open my own studio. It's amazing how much stuff you need when you're too egocentric to even consider the room he had to make for me and my baggage, psychic and otherwise.

Straight away, romance vanished. I felt like I was in some kind of bad MTV video. David shifted into performance mode and became distant. It was like he evaporated into another, frankly way less fun version of himself. He was moody and quiet, saving his voice for his fans. I was keen on going to new places; he'd been there before, to all of them, several times, so I went sightseeing by myself because he was conserving his energy for the show. I felt more like a mistress than a wife. He was married first and foremost to Music and on tour he was Serious Business. I felt isolated and alone, regretful of ditching my happy yoga life for *him*. Resentment started creeping in, muddying the waters and complicating everything. I was starting to not like the man I had dropped everything for to get closer to. I also started to understand what Queen Victoria meant when she said, "I would venture to warn against too great an intimacy with artists, as it is very seductive and a little dangerous."

I knew David was the real deal. I've known it since the first five seconds of meeting him. His authenticity is one of the things I love about him most. What I didn't know until I saw it on tour was the depth of his earnestness, his utter devotion to his craft. I underestimated the energy he puts forth; the custodial honor he feels about Music. His love of sharing songs is so clear and enormous it becomes a high ceremony just to witness him putting his soul on the line night after night. You wouldn't necessarily see these fine details unless you get close, which is why his concerts are events of the heart. David's art is quiet, which is a funny way to describe a rock show unless you see a man like David on stage, whose spirit meets his bones the second the music starts. Our venues are mainly and deliberately performing arts theaters, where we, the audience, are near enough to see him sweat. Passion drips off him in such a way we feel invited to sit *with* him, not passively observe him from the other side of the curtain. His concerts aren't an act. His work is who he is.

Acquaintances ask me why he "made me" come on tour with him, but my real friends understand he invited me into his world. For a public person, David is intensely private. Music is inseparable from his soul, and a call to tour with him was a proposal to be a part of his heart. I didn't know it then but I sure know it now—had I not gone out on tour I would have missed practically everything profound about him.

But those early days of touring were rough. There was an unexpected heaviness to the love triangle between David, Music, and me. Having just jumped on board I could hardly deal with what felt like a whole other person riding on the bus with us. I was even a little jealous of her. I mean, how do you compete with *that*? My usual crutches—great clothes, manicured hands, witty banter—weren't working. My cutest fringe jacket didn't even turn his head.

Saucha is described as purity and I was anything but pure of heart. It wasn't long before I wanted him to go straight to hell because he didn't even acknowledge how put together I was. Did he not understand how hard it was to blow dry my hair when my elbow kept banging against the bathroom mirror? Did he not realize how trying it was to put on mascara as the bus wheels hit potholes? Did he not see all the effort I put into looking pretty? Nope. He just ate his cereal and left his bowl in the sink and returned to the dungeon of his Music. Which just happened to be three feet away from where I was trying to wiggle into a pair of BDG high-waisted jeans.

Saucha also means interacting with others with those unsoiled, sparkling hearts. Whatever. On that first tour, I was sure I was stuck in Buddha's first noble truth, that Life is Suffering. I wasn't swept off my feet by a spontaneous stop at a used bookstore in a Seattle downpour, as I'd so clearly pictured it as I packed for the tour. Nor did my heart—clean or not—soar into the sky as David asked our driver to pull over on a foggy, Northern California cove for a seemingly-impromptu but expertly planned picnic. As David revised one song and then another, as he took his vow of silence to prep his vocal chords for his followers, I sulked. I wasn't having *any* fun. The steely quiet on the bus was hardly solace from the noise and crowds and chaos and pressure we encountered when we stepped off of it.

Nothing was cozy, nothing was romantic, and my heart wasn't having it. Hafiz said, "Love creates a home whoever it is. Love is never in want. True love is always in a state of found." I felt found, alright. A fool who fell for her own this-is-how-great-the-tour-will-be fantasy.

Four weeks into that first tour, while David was on stage in concert, I covered up our merch table and fled to our bus where I could be alone to hatch a plan of escape. *Can you annul an agreement to go on tour with your husband?* I thought. Couldn't I just, I don't know, resume the life we'd had—the one where I saw him only a couple of times a month, every few months, where he untethered himself from Music's seductive pull before he entered our Ojai house? What's more economical—Expedia or Travelocity? Scratch that; who cares: Where's the first plane that can take me back to California?

But once inside the Prevost, I took stock of where I was. It was the only home, like it or not, accessible. The TV was blaring Bad News. The bedsheets were rumpled from David's pre-show nap. Freshly-laundered clothes were hanging over the bunk. Dirty clothes were stacked on the sofa, begging to be washed. The refrigerator and cabinets were smudged with fingerprints, even handprints, all of them sticky and oily from who-knows-what. David's dining table was a madhouse of papers containing phone interview numbers, half-finished lyrics, and lists of restaurants to visit. Guitar pics peppered the surface, intermixed with a smattering of spilled almonds and an empty carton of coconut water. The floor was a landmine of dog food and road dirt, and hairy dust-balls glared at me from the corners. The air held a stale stench, just like what you'd think a working tour bus would smell like: sweat mixed with takeout and bad breath.

I've been afraid of anything that resembles housework since I almost burned my childhood house down with my Suzy Homemaker Easy Bake Oven. To this day, I've never seen my mother as terrified as she was running out into the backyard with my pink oven aflame. The whole experience upset her so badly any domestic work whatsoever still makes me nervous. As silly as it sounds, I'm afraid of doing it all wrong. That evening on tour, I was sure I was doing my whole

Already

healed,

already

whole.

✣ *Tibetian Mantra*

life wrong. I had a feeling of tension in my stomach, a tightness in my heart, a shortness of breath. I knew these markers and the story they told. The one that read *you are not lovable* and *your life is a big mess*.

And for the first time ever, I wanted to scour this from my mind. I wanted to rise above it.

I stood tall in that bus and owned it. I rolled up my tour t-shirt sleeves and started cleaning. I didn't care that I didn't know what I was doing; I just knew it needed doing. As the bus began to take on an orderly vibe, I started to delight in my newfound job as bus maid. Cleaning a tour bus is my kind of housekeeping because it really doesn't take much. A little dusting and sweeping and folding a few clothes is all it takes; it's the perfect amount to help me feel like a wife taking care of her man without compromising my feminist streak. I don't often cook, bake, or sew; I'm not a great vacuumer. But, I thought, I can handle domesticity on this bus like a goddamned goddess.

It only took thirty minutes to make the bed, fold the clothes, start the wash, organize David's table, and wipe down the entire 45-foot interior surface. I diffused the air with organic oils, dimmed the lights, and switched the TV to the blues station. Leaving the bus in a triumphant blaze of glory, I reentered the theater just in time to reopen merch (which, by the way, is always well-manicured and orderly).

Marie Kondo says the objective of cleaning is not just to clean, but to feel happiness living within that environment. The yoga sutras say happiness is the very byproduct of cleanliness. We usually live in an externally-oriented, appearance-focused world. The real work wasn't about cleaning the bus. It was about making a choice to be grateful for my life and the man who invited me into his. It was me who actually got a huge dose of cleaning, and to my amazement, the bus started to feel like home. Add a little love to a relationship, even with a bus, and everything, and I mean everything, starts to improve.

Rumi said, "There are a thousand ways to kneel and kiss the earth." There are also a thousand ways to show love and a thousand ways to do ustrasana, or camel pose. Just ask a thousand teachers because everybody teaches it a little differently. But there's one thing almost every yogi agrees upon: Camel is one of the most important backbends you can practice, the one you should commit to daily. It's stilling, eye-opening, and cathartic. Opening your heart always is.

In camel pose, your knees are grounded on earth, while your neck—home to your Vishuddha, or throat, chakra—bends back. Until you're comfy in it, it's an uncomfortable, even petrifying pose, presenting challenges that range from straining your cervical spine to generating shooting pain in your sacrum. But the beauty of it, as well as the terror, is that it forces you to look back—at the choices you've made that have brought you here and what you are capable of as you push your hips forward. It asks you to remain calm and pure while all of you is open, fragile, and dependent on the strength of your other parts.

I've spent years carrying shame because I don't make a mean casserole. Add to this is the fact that, unlike the Wilson women before me, I don't mend socks. I don't iron sheets. Ingrained in me from my childhood is the unfaltering belief that a good housekeeper, personal or paid, is required to be a good woman. Disgrace is foul and sticky, and I swear it lives in my lower back. Ustrasana awakens it, and reminds me that I'm still tender when it comes to my confidence in what it means to be a domestic queen, or a patient, loving wife.

The same fear I feel when I drop back into camel was with me as I made my way to the bus after the merch booth closed after the show. I felt a freefall in self-assurance, uncertain if I had the strength to keep up with this tour, this husband to whom I became invisible as he wrote lyrics, this life. *Did I clean the bus right?* I asked myself. Should I have not touched his sacred, artistic place? Why am I walking around a parking lot at midnight in the rain and not fast asleep at home? It doesn't matter how many showers you take: Unclean thoughts can contaminate anything.

I trudged up the four steep steps on the bus and peered in. Through the moody lights and the haze of our newly-sweet smelling space, I saw David sitting in his usual, post-concert spot, our dog

Let the beauty of what you love be what you do. There are a thousand ways to kneel and kiss the ground, there are a thousand ways to go home again.

— Rumi

Lucy in one arm and a glass of wine in the other. His stage towel was wrapped around his neck. He looked like a cube of ice thawing out from the aloof, Music-obsessed Dave. His blue eyes met mine, and a new voice, one different from the one he uses only for other people, cracked in graciousness as he said, "Thank you." It was the first authentic connection I'd felt on the whole tour. *Ah!* I thought. He's different tonight. Maybe there's hope after all.

The biggest change wasn't in him, though. It was in me.

It seems all these years I've had it backward; that I've been sanitizing the wrong spots. You don't do things to make people love you. You love who you are, and from there connection happens. I'm the one I've been waiting for to come home. Rumi said it best when he remarked that "what you seek is seeking you." Everything that you want, you already are.

The *Bhagavad Gita* tells us that Arjuna, in the heat of a battle, said, "No learning can happen without love." I'm seeing that the learning to love happens in the small print of everyday life. I'm learning about housekeeping, like it really does help to separate the light from the dark when doing laundry. I'm also learning to love doing my part to make David happy and his tour a little smoother. But mainly I'm learning that feeling unlovable is pure deception. The sutras call these "veils" on the heart because they block our view of the truth. Learning and love and intimacy start by looking at your own heart and taking responsibility for how you show up in the world. What kind of heart are you carrying around? What kind of heart did I pack for this trip? Mother Theresa said "do small things with great love" because when learning such big lessons like how to love you gotta start where you are and with what you have, even if an unkempt tour bus is your only available tool.

Love songs are always almost written about others. Rumor has it Steven Stills was missing his girlfriend while on tour with Crosby, Stills & Nash in London, probably pouting around backstage like we all do when we're heavy-hearted, when a fellow tour mate, soul singer Doris Troy, said, "Love the one you're with." We all miss this simple, universal spiritual truth: To look at what's right in front of us and love purely anyway. It's an acceptance, not necessarily an agreement. It's a tuning in, not a tuning out. It's a skillset of alignment with your own heart first, not the storybook fantasy you've imagined.

Now, I clean the bus every show night as a practice of *saucha*. At first, I did it because I knew it pleased David. It was a pragmatic, blatant practice of loving the one I was with. As the bus and my motives of trying to win love became cleaner, so did the path of responsibility for my own alignment. I'm the person I'm with the most, actually. Can I love myself? Baba Ram Dass said, "When I need love from others, or need to give love to others, I'm caught in an unstable situation. Being love, rather than giving or taking love, is the only thing that provides stability. Being love means seeing the Beloved all around me." This is no simple task, of course. But a clean view of the road sure makes it easier.

Strength

Shanti Vitabhadrasana
Peaceful Warrior

4

Shine On You Crazy Diamond

Day 96 of our summer tour and in a rare find of a yoga class that fits our demanding schedule, I'm enjoying every moment. Not that yoga doesn't make demands in her own way. The word for practice is *abyhasa* and sutra 1.14 makes it clear that it requires constancy: "But that practice only becomes firmly established when it has been executed with great attention and without interruption over a long period of time." How am I supposed to endeavor all this while living my life—and touring with a rock-and-roll band? Funny thing is, I'm realizing I don't have to choose between yoga and touring. There isn't a separation between a spiritual and material life, just as there isn't a separation between your foot and your mind. It's all one body.

I'm flipping over my toes, vinyasa style, from updog to downdog, during this innocent class in the middle of a long tour. I'm freer than I've been in weeks. But today I see something new: My right foot dragging seconds behind my left. The word that comes to mind—and it just pops in there, as if it descended from heaven above—is *weak*. Lazy, even.

As a recovering Type A, I sort of love this self-imposed label, but if it's not serving my right hip, it's not serving my downdog, and come to think of it, it's not serving my half-moon or my handstand either. I'm operating under the illusion that if I correct this little hitch in my hip all these poses will become easy, which is essentially the equivalent of thinking that life would be cake if I could just lose those last five pounds/buy my dream house/score that gig/insert your "if only" here. Besides: Yoga isn't about the poses. The late Viniyoga master T.K.V. Desikachar said, "The success of yoga does not lie in the ability to perform postures, but in how it positively changes the way we live our life and our relationships."

He's not the only one who maintains this. Yoga is a discipline to assist us in the journey of our lives, foster awareness, and restore our sanity. I've been on the brink of mine more than once while touring. In Patanjali's Yoga Sutras, the path is comprised of eight steps that serve as guidelines to live a meaningful and purposeful life, with suggestions about moral conduct and self-discipline, attention toward one's health, and a tuning-in to the spiritual aspects of our nature. The Latin root of the word discipline is *peodscipe*, meaning "treatment that corrects or punishes" from the notion of "order necessary for instruction." Meaning, there must be some internal order, some inclination or desire, so that the *real* teachings of yoga can land. My weakness, really, isn't so much in my right hip. It's in my quickness to feel less than and inferior to the rest of the team; my tendency towards shame and despair in being the odd man—or in my case, woman—out on the road.

I first heard Pink Floyd in high school. The guys I hung out with were the tastemakers in our group; they had say over what record spun on the turntable during our smoke-filled house parties. I was the odd woman out then as well—I hadn't yet caught on to the brilliance of "Wish You Were Here." I was vocal about it too, which garnered a lot of eye-rolls, especially when I'd request Steve Miller's "The Joker" for the fifth time or Lynyrd Skynrd's "Sweet Home Alabama" for the millionth time. My music proclivities, apparently, were so last year.

The only exception to this was "Shine On You Crazy Diamond." Written by David Gilmour, it was a tribute to Syd Barrett, a cofounder of Pink Floyd who was kicked out of the band because of his heavy drug use and erratic behavior.

When you're working with a band, or any group for that matter, it's about teamwork, and a weak link—let alone one suffering from addiction and a mental illness—brings the whole operation to a grinding halt. I've had to lean in to the practices of yoga, to build strength of body, but even more crucial, of character, lest I too follow the same fate as Mr. Barrett. To blend into Dave's band, I've had to up my game and trade some grace for grit. There's no room for laziness anywhere.

Post-show, when the rest of the band unwinds, is show-time for me. We are the busiest at our booth after the concert. The fans have been whipped into a frenzy, having risen from their seats several times for standing ovations throughout the concert and been on their feet during the entirety of the two-song encore. By the time they hit the merch booth, they're wild with delight and eager to tell you all about…well, just about anything, really. It's the rock-and-roll Wild West stretched over two folding tables, and as quickly as the crowds appear, it all comes to a sudden stop and I'm left standing alone at the merch table shaking my head from their onslaught of enthusiasm and joy.

All that energy strikes like a tidal wave. I get swept up every single time and it's thrilling, completely thrilling. A Herculean effort of sorts is required to withstand that many people and that much excitement, and only doable because the fans hold me up. In fact, it's a little lonely once everybody leaves. It's just me and the leftover merchandise. We are both strewn in every direction, the CDs and albums, the t-shirts and baseball hats, all these things that, one by one, must be carefully counted, reorganized, restacked, and refolded before placing them in their cases.

This isn't like packing a Samsonite Ultralight suitcase for a weekend in The Hamptons. We use what's called "road cases." Developed by the airline industry, they're sturdily-constructed, oversized containers based on airplane parts able to withstand the rigors of being shipped hundreds of times. They're guaranteed to survive, undamaged, over multiple flights. These massive wonders of engineering are a lot stronger than I am, and I've spent many midnights staring at them in a psychic showdown, wondering which one is going to drop first from the weight of what she carries.

Once packed and snapped shut, it's hauling time, the biggest burden of all. The heavy cases don't just walk themselves back to the bus. Quality wheels aside, someone must heave them upright and roll them down long hallways and up staircases, through dark alleyways and past blinding bus headlights. It's work that must be done. It can never be avoided, whether you feel like it or not, and many nights I'm on the side of not.

I've had to develop new muscles to do the physical work of merchandising. I've crossed a threshold of physical pain. I've had to sweat. But what I've had to do more than anything is cultivate a surefooted belief system about what it means to be a woman.

For most of my life, I've kept my strength—literal and metaphorical—underdeveloped, misaligned in the conviction that strength compromises femininity. The new muscles in my biceps and thighs—from running around venues and lifting heavy cases—has me looking more roadie than debutante these days. Many nights (too many), I've tried to move weighty boxes by batting my eyelashes and offering free t-shirts and bending just so. I've failed to summon a single stage crew. Getting passed over, I feel middle-aged and totally ridiculous in my leopard jeans, fringe jacket, and sparkly sandals. My tired body regards this as a blow; my ego is gutted.

The truth is, I'm no longer a young woman. I know we're all beautiful in God's eyes but let's be real: The beauty of a young woman moves this material world in downright potent ways. Even Buddha, on his way to enlightenment, was tempted by Mara appearing as a young woman. To which Buddha is rumored to have said, "If there was a force stronger than sex, I wouldn't have made it."

I see the effects of aging in yoga, in my cranky hips and in my inner thighs, which aren't so perky anymore. My dangling triceps look like my grandmother's arms. All of these changes seem so private and subtle that I can deceive myself into thinking that aging isn't happening to me at all. But having men refuse my plea for help with merch boxes? It feels like the death of the beautiful young Winifred. It's also confirmation that I can no longer depend on my youth for help, or more specifically, to convince someone else to do the hard work for me.

Since my twenties, I've let men do the heavy lifting, everything from a sack of groceries to paying the lion's share of the bills to making me feel worthy and meaningful and "whole." Some of this was learned from my family, some of it comes from images lifted from *Vogue*, but most of it comes from an unexamined, slow leak of giving away my own power.

Ravi Ravindra says yoga isn't about understanding the truth; it's about withstanding it. When a profound realization hits you, you have to be strong enough to take it, process it, and learn from it. Sutra 2.23 says, "The inability to discern between the temporary, fluctuating mind and our own true Self, which is eternal, is the cause of our suffering, yet this suffering provides us with the opportunity to make this distinction and to learn and grow from it, by understanding the true nature of each."

I've been blind to true beauty for most of my life. But now that I'm older, I'm starting to see it isn't in a symmetrical Michelle Pfeiffer face, or high cheekbones, or taut thighs. It's in qualities that are impervious to the years slipping by: Kindness. Dedication. Wisdom. Humor and intelligence and compassion and resilience. I've been lazy when it comes to my own self-reliance because I spent too many years cultivating the external appearance of myself instead of bolstering these timeless traits. I've played the young pretty thing card for as long as possible, and right there in that cold concert hall I have to fess up to myself and say, the game is over, girl. "Beauty is a short lived tyranny," anyway—or so Socrates said. Life and yoga, it seems, are conspiring to help me see things differently.

During a tour, there's no better way to be reminded of what's at stake in the whirlwind of life than taking a yoga class. It's a reprieve from the tour world; some distance to gain perspective. Strong standing poses feel empowering; a place to discover confidence from within.

Shanti Virabhadrasana—or Peaceful Warrior—is one of them. It sounds like an oxymoron at first. How can you be strong and serene at once? But yoga lore is filled with battle scenes. The last line in many Bhagavad Gita chapters is the demand that we "stand up and fight." A warrior's strength is revered not as an "us against them" but as an "us against ourselves." The call is to battle the universal enemy, self-ignorance—or avidya—which is a well-spring for major grief.

Many warrior poses have an even balance to them, but Peaceful Warrior requires a certain asymmetry. One must stay grounded in the legs, feet firmly planted on the earth, while the heart tilts off center. Both arms are extended long, one internally rotating on the stability of your outstretched leg, the other externally, in a gesture of opening to higher energies. The heart gets wringed out and finds balance in the midst of this contained, taxing, and graceful lopsidedness. Practice evolves with a spiraling action in the heart, and with it arrives greater insights. Peaceful Warrior exemplifies both power and tranquility—in short, what it means to be a woman today.

What holds the pose steady is the navel center, home to the Manipura chakra, our energetic center of self-esteem, sense of purpose, and personal identity. One translation of this chakra is "city filled with jewels." I've always loved imagining this. At our center, it seems to say, we are diamond-like, precious, abundantly beautiful, and clear in mind and body. But, while diamonds are the hardest naturally-occurring material known, they also have structural weaknesses. We, too, have hurts that destabilize us. Diamond cutting is tricky. Life is even trickier.

The steadiness of Peaceful Warrior is also her most vulnerable. The Manipura takes most of the pressure. Not so much the front belly, the part that's easy to see, the part that's exposed to the light, but the harder-to-see lower back, right where the adrenals sit like little party hats on top of our kidneys; right where, the yogis say, we store our fear. It takes physical strength and mental courage to lift this area of the body, but it takes *massive* discipline to not listen to the voice that says "you're not strong enough, beautiful enough, young enough; you're not enough of anything." The word *tapas*, part of ashtanga's *niyama* (or self-observances), instructs ways to triumph over this sort of thinking: discipline, heat, desire; deep strength required to burn off impurities. And just like heat transforms water to vapor, the pose, and all yoga, alchemizes every aspect of life if we discipline ourselves to follow her instructions.

Diamonds are hugely esteemed, their beauty and purity revered by their ability to reflect light. Metaphysics say diamonds bring a clear, positive resolution to all that ails us, especially after we have become willing to admit our wrong perceptions and approaches. A mind able to do this is referred to as the "diamond mind" in the yoga sutras.

Diamonds are the chosen gem for wedding rings, including mine, which is the reason I am where I am on this path— and why I'm sitting in a freezing concert hall wishing I had enough muscle to lug these merch cases where they need to go.

Sutra 2.46 is one of the few references in ancient texts regarding poses. It says *"sthira sukkham asanam,* a pose is strong and firm, and also has ease." It's often cited as a suggestion to bring effortlessness into your exertions. But the Sutra can tilt backwards, like the heart in Peaceful Warrior, and ask us to bring some effort into relaxing in our daily battles with our own self, to stop fighting life so much, including my petty concern for my once-toned arms and legs and wrinkle-free face—the looks that got men to do the heavy lifting in my life.

What's required is a willingness to live our truth, a steadfast determination to shine our own light from within. The ego gets such a bad rap in yoga, but a strong ego is essential for anything to happen. The first word in the Rig Veda is *agni,* or fire. It's a burning desire for inner stillness and spiritual strength so we can show up in the world in the best possible version of ourselves. "Sparkling like a diamond" isn't a lukewarm action. It's a fire from within.

Marianne Williamson says, "Our deepest fear isn't our darkness, it's our light. Who are we not to be fabulous?" This is the kind of question that turns a cold concert lobby into a temple. It's the kind of question I'm not sure we can know, but the important thing is it puts us in the direction of the diamond mind. In the Brihadaranyaka Upanishad there is a myth whereby Gargi is warned to not ask too many questions lest her head fall off. It seems we are only allowed to see enough truth so that our heads don't explode. There's just enough to nourish us when we need it the most.

Rilke, meanwhile, encourages us to live the questions. "Perhaps you will then gradually, without noticing it, live along some distant day into the answer." In this moment, with my muscles and ego aching, I realize that I can start heading towards this distant day. I can, as Pink Floyd once sang, remember when I was young and shone like the sun. It's a choice, this willingness to strive, and one that takes strength and diligence. Marriage and touring, it seems, are some of my biggest teachers for learning resilience and boundaries and the capacity to expand. They limit my more careless ways, while bringing clarity to the power of consistent, focused efforts to be part of, not separate *than*. To be part of the band. To be someone's other half. To be a part of a community. To be a part of someone's night out at a performance. They inspire me to practice and not be so crazy. They also laugh a lot when I am.

It's half past midnight after a later-than-usual show. I'm beyond tired and ready for bed. I'd rather be hanging out with my dog and a good book. I stare at the two heavy tour cases and an overstuffed briefcase that needs to be hauled to the bus. I've asked for help three times but nobody has shown up. The heat within shifts from anger to fuel. The real battle isn't against the men who've dominated my life, but against my own foolish choices. Against my unwavering belief that I, alone, am not enough. Getting angry or wanting it to be different isn't yoga. Being fabulous and shiny bright is, and it takes every ounce of strength I can muster.

I take a breath and summon my inner power, the one I had lost and given away and downplayed for so many years. I bend my knees and kneel down and grab that heavy-ass case and drag it to the bus. I deliver it with a thank you, and go back for the second load, because that's what life is asking me to do right now. Every step of this little task requires muscle to stay on the path; every breath confirms where I'm headed. This is the discipline, this is the heat, these are the moments of a Peaceful Warrior.

Surrender

Balasana
Child's Pose

5

Landslide

I bought Fleetwood Mac's *Rumors* before I heard a single song because I loved the way Stevie Nicks looked on the cover. To be more specific, it was her clothes that captivated me. A cape and ballet shoes seemed so daring, so free. She struck me, in 1977, as the most beautiful woman in the world.

What I didn't know then is that surface beauty, or the lack of it, is a small-hearted way of seeing the world. I'm convinced that judging a book by its cover, or in this case, a record, is learned behavior—and one I was exceptionally good at for years. Like many women, this translated into body image issues. Until I discovered yoga, my body was tricky territory—unreliable at best, uninhabited in the truest sense, and under ruthless scrutiny. I held myself accountable to high standards of perfection, and inflicted both subtle and merciless harm on the very thing that allowed me to move through the world. The pressure I put on myself was bottomless.

For years, I lived one layer up—outside of my own skin and swathed in fabulous clothes, like a mannequin on display. Fashion shielded me from shame and wrapped me in confidence. Stevie Nicks was a constant source of inspiration; she wore clothes better than just about anyone. Her album spent more time on my dressing table than my turntable, propped up alongside my double-sided, day-to-evening lighted Maybelline mirror. I'd cake on eyeliner, just to look like her, all the while wishing I had the guts to wear something as cool as she did. I was in high school at the time, drowning in a conservative Texan culture, where allowing girls to wear pants on Fridays was considered forward thinking. I had to save my bell bottoms for weekend wear, when I'd attempt to look like Stevie with my peasant blouses cinched at the waist and wide and flowing at the wrists.

Beautiful clothes implied connection with others because it was early currency with my mother. I was five when I did my first fashion show at Neiman Marcus. Although I was too little and too innocent to know a thing about designer labels, I wasn't too young to realize that attention and self-worth could arrive through your appearance. In the end, I picked up a lifelong obsession with beauty on a makeshift runway at the Zodiac Room in downtown Dallas.

How bewildering and enticing it was that with a change of an outfit came a change in attentiveness and a sense of being popular, even loved. As soon as my ordinary play clothes were traded in for Neiman Marcus's stylish attire, a flurry of excitement and a fussing over of what I was becoming took hold. Dressed and made up, I was, somehow, bigger, more vital. Who knew shiny patent leather shoes and little white ankle socks could make a room full of moms swoon? I felt like a princess in a petticoat; I swished around that dressing room making the sounds of ocean waves. A pink sweater with real pearls made my mother's head tilt sideways in reverence—a memorable gesture, given that she herself was gorgeous and immaculately-dressed. Her elegant clothes never held her back from hugging me—even when I'd come home from a day of bike riding, creek exploring, or tree fort building—but that day was the first time I noticed actual admiration in her eyes. She taught me that looks don't really matter but I couldn't trust these words from a woman who turned heads everywhere we went.

The fashion show was the greatest dress-up day of all until I was stuffed into an overcoat that confined my arms and outfitted in a matching hat, angled atop my head in such a way that I could barely see out of my left eye. It didn't feel right. It was disorienting and weird, and before I could get my bearings, and under tremendous protest, I was ushered out the door and into a big ballroom with ritzy chandeliers, where I was made to walk, choking on tears, down a runway framed by people dining at white-clothed tables serviced by gloved butlers. You could feel the judgment through the thin cloud of cigarette smoke; hear it in the forks tapping the fine china. I frantically searched for my mother as I walked through the room—something that was rarely difficult, given her beauty. I was trying to catch her kind blue eyes, but staring back were only hardened squints from unfamiliar faces, critical and intense. They pierced right through me. They gave me a lesson.

In the years that followed, wearing the "right" clothes became a way to escape the dread of never being enough. It took decades to see that any time you try to dress up your insides by acquiring something outside you're in a no-win situation. By the time I made it to my first yoga class in 2003, I had an enormous closet—a boudoir, really, equipped with its own ritzy chandelier. It was filled to bursting with clothes. Since the age of five I'd crammed my dreams and desires so deep in my body that self-expression only felt safe through the attire that hung in my closet, the space like a shrine. Most of those clothes never actually got worn. Rather, they hung as reminders of everything I was not; of a self that still needed fixing.

My closet was also the first place where I began to drink in secret. In my thirties and early forties, I'd make it through the day as an executive, come home to our big, beautiful house, have dinner with my husband, and, while he retired in front of the television for the evening, continue sipping expensive white wine well past midnight with my clothes, wondering if the evening gowns around me were as lonely as their owner. Sometimes I'd try things on, carefully slipping dresses and skirts and tops off their hangers while fantasizing about where I would wear them. In those dazzling garments, I went to a presidential inauguration, walked the red carpet with Robert Duvall, sipped cognac après ski in Gstaad, boarded my private jet to Rio. An outfit for every big life plan, which, of course, exactly none of which were happening at the time because I was clinging to an image of what kept me loveable and drinking myself away behind closed doors. I'd locked myself into that closet, so to speak, and couldn't find my way out.

By sharp contrast, when I started going to yoga, I did so in utilitarian and unflattering tank tops and stretchy pants. The heat melted away my makeup and any semblance of silky hair. There was no glamour; no attempts at perfection. It busted my idealized self to shreds.

The landslide of my divorce changed everything even more. When I left my marriage a lot of my clothes didn't make the trip, partly because of the physical effort of having to move them, partly because of the psychic surrender that had me in her grips. I didn't know who I was supposed to be underneath all those clothes. What do people wear in Ojai, anyway? Admitting a leopard Dolce & Gabbana gown really didn't fit right and some Prada pumps hurt my feet may sound trivial to some, but they were the fragile first steps towards trusting myself, as the relinquishing of them forced me to examine my inner life. "The question of what you want to own is actually the question of how you want to live your life," Marie Kondo says in *The Life-Changing Magic of Tidying Up*. I knew I wanted to find a way to be comfortable in my own skin, and at that point even my most expensive clothes felt agonizing. High heels hurt my feet. My leather handbags felt like gym weights. Sequined tops were scratchy, and those flowy Stevie Nicks' sleeves I still wore decades later just got dragged over dinner plates and were anything but sexy once soiled by mashed potatoes. I'm convinced part of the reason I became a yogi was because those were the only clothes my body could tolerate.

Now, my life is more Birkenstocks than ball gowns, and the only spandex I own is in my Lululemons. But even through all my practices, there is a binging and purging constantly at work in my closet, a conveyer belt of clothes coming in and going out.

On tour with David, my shopping habit has no place to hide. Our tour bus barely has any closet at all. I actually measured it once. I have 36 and a half inches of hanging space, plus a secret compartment under the bed that can fit 12 pairs of shoes (jam is more like it).

And yet, as the tour gets rolling, I accumulate clothes along the way. Shopping becomes armor against the wear and tear of late nights, stale air, restaurant food, and the occasional sense of being invisible and on display at once. New clothes smell fresh and full of potential; they feel like a balmy salve.

Until, suddenly, they didn't.

If I'd have been paying closer attention I would have noticed these little trips to various boutiques had begun to shift from exercises in pleasure to missions of shame. I'd sneak back on the bus with my bags and shove my pretty new clothes in the office supply drawer like a reflex. As the interior bus space began to overflow, I'd slink into the bus belly, her merch bay, and crawl back behind our active inventory to fill stock containers to the brim. Empty guitar cases turned into suitcases; the contents of Tupperware containers were pitched to accommodate my new cashmere sweaters.

My relationship with bus clothes is so intimate, we are such good friends, that I can usually tell exactly what pair of pants or which jacket is in my hands just by touch. This skill comes in handy on show nights when Dave naps before performing. In an effort to let him sleep, I tiptoe in the dark and open the closet just enough to reach in and feel what outfit I'll wear. Getting dressed by Braille has made for some bizarre combinations, which often makes me feel even more uncomfortable and out of place on an already demanding evening. At times the closet has simply been inaccessible before a show and I'm forced to show up "as is." For someone who identifies strongly with racks of expensive clothes just waiting for someone to love them back, "as is" is a terrifying reminder that something is irreparably flawed, possibly with hidden holes. Not worth top price.

Mild panic ensues on those nights especially. Tour life moves fast and the lifetime of stories I've clothed myself in gets tossed out quicker than I can add a fresh new layer. Cities don't look like I've pictured them, fans don't always behave as I wished they would, band mates show me sides I'd rather not see. I need protection from these things, and so I call upon old behaviors. At one point, the bus was positively overflowing with clothes; I'd shopped in almost every major U.S. city, and still, I couldn't control the only way I once knew how to soothe myself: With clothes, clothes, and more clothes.

Yoga, however, is all about showing up "as is." Teachings declare the conditions in our life *right now* are exactly what we need to help us wake up, show up, and grow up. We must surrender the thought that whatever is happening right now should not be. In this context, surrender is referred to as Ishvara Pranidad. It's a capitulation and dedication to Supreme Being and a Higher Self.

No pose epitomizes what's required of this like balasana, or child's pose. The nature of child's pose is a turning inward. Placement of the head connects to the earth, calming one's mental chatter in service to the higher wisdom of the heart. The back of the neck, so used to holding it all together, begins to relax, right at the base of the skull, where the parasympathetic nerve lives. The belly, intestines, spleen, and liver all soften towards the ground, completely protected, while the kidneys, said to store the energy of fear, puff up and air out with each breath. Legs folded in support of the heart stops us from running in circles in the same old patterns, the chasing after the illusive *more more more*, and instead asks us to acknowledge the gifts we already have. Our big toes touch, containing our life force, and we breathe in recognition of the life force within us. Deeply relaxing into who we are below the surface, naked or clothed, happy or sad—in short, *as is*—is the key to surrender.

All of this is important. The ego thrives on *not enough*. It reinforces scarcity—personal and otherwise. It tells us we're not good enough, don't do enough, haven't accomplished enough, aren't pretty enough, aren't slender enough, don't have the right clothes. It shrinks us, collapsing us into what yogis call *asmita*, or a sense of a separate self, disconnected from the all-loving, all-sufficient source. As we surrender to truth, we see we have everything we need for our journey in this lifetime, no immense closet required.

Balasana is a quiet—and challenging—pose. Surrender has a bad taste because of its implication of giving up, and the mechanics of child's pose forces us to face ourselves. But surrendering permits us to drop hardened layers of protection. New levels of freedom are accessed; new comfort in just being ourselves in this sacred world is felt. We see we *are* enough. As is.

Child's pose is called upon in yoga classes to allow us to catch our breath, often after a difficult standing sequence, just as the purpose of surrender in life is to maintain contact with our real self in the frenzy of daily existence, through the untiring distractions of things and thoughts and feelings. The Isa Upanishad says, "The entire world is the garment of the Lord." I interpret this as a call to surrender to the Divine Grace that has you in her hold and clothes you in human form right here on Mother Earth; to let go of striving to find perfection Out There because it's already Right Here. Why search for designer labels when we ourselves are perfectly designed?

In time, the solution for making more room in my closets was absurdly simple: To stop adding more clothes to it. There wasn't really a problem regarding closet space; it required a landslide, a whole world of thought to tumble down. *If you see my reflection in a snow covered hill, will a landslide bring it down?* is a good question when you live in the mountains; it's a great question when you have mountains of clothes in your possession and realize they don't make you happy. That, rather, "happiness is the nature of the self," as Ramana Mahrishi reminds us.

So what happened to all my clothes? There was no sweeping landslide whereby I removed them from the nooks and crannies and Tupperware containers; ditched them once and for all. Are you crazy? I love clothes, and probably always will. But I don't need them like I used to. I don't hide behind them out of fear of not being loved, or deemed worthy. I enjoy them as a way to live life full-on, declaring my unique expression, my joyous place in the divine dance of it all.

Faith

Hanumanasana
Monkey Pose

6

Don't Stop Believin'

I'm a flexie with my hamstrings these days. Maybe it's from those years of ballet classes not long after I learned to walk, maybe it's a hangover from high school cheerleading. Or maybe it's inbred; runs in the family. Whatever the case may be, I love a deep, solid, back-of-the-leg stretch. It makes me feel capable and strong. Gloriously graceful.

But along with my bendy hamstrings, I've also inherited deep-seated southern etiquette from a long line of pretty, polite women. These ladies and I: We run on the distinctively feminine rules of the house, and have the façade to go with it: Seemingly uncomplicated. Impeccably mannered. Unremittingly put-together.

I'm the only daughter of three children. My mother was an only daughter of two; my maternal grandmother was an only child. My father's side hadn't seen a female offspring in decades until me. His brother had a beauty eight years after me, and she is about as perfect of a woman as you'd ever want to meet. Given how few females were in my family, the pressure to represent our sex well was tremendous. I was born in 1961, a pivotal decade for American women, and I'm not sure my parents knew what to do with me. In the midst of bra-burning and women's-libbing, much of my Dallas upbringing was focused on the trifling details of "proper" living. Such as how to host dinner parties.

I can set a table, full service, practically in my sleep. I know the dinner fork is between the salad and dessert fork, the butter dish is on the left, and the glassware is on the right. I prefer the napkin centered on top of the salad plate, secured by an elegant ring—it seems much more artful than simply folded on the left side of the dinner plate. This attention to detail makes sense, in retrospect: In my family there was incredible fuss over a formally-arranged table, as if the precision of a plate could ensure a successful party. I silently wondered about the deeper question—*what about the actual food? The company?*—but never had the confidence to challenge the generational rules of decorum.

The system seemed to work well until one evening when one of our guests—by far, the most beautiful and refined woman at our whole party—got drunk and threw a glass of fine French red wine on her husband. I remember thinking I'd done something wrong with my place settings, but quickly brushed off the thought: It was too devastating to lose faith in the longstanding table wisdom passed down to us Wilson women.

All of this has helped me be a sensitive dinner guest. I show up on time and eat what's dished up. I don't throw wine, at least anymore. And all this social training, all these rules and manners, serve me well as a traveling yogi too.

Having attended hundreds of yoga classes in different studios around the country, I've come to have faith in the practice, that it will be great, no matter if it's served up vigorous or gentle; in a heated room or outside; mat-to-mat crowded or attended by just a few. Part of my yoga practice starts before I even get to a studio: I make sure to arrive in plenty of time to sign in, acclimatize to the studio, and set up my space with a mat, water bottle, blanket, strap, and a couple of blocks.

This is the politeness I've been fed since childhood. It's also the *ritual of a pleasant experience*. In my own quiet way, I slip in and out of studios around the country like a well-appointed table awaiting her main course.

So you can imagine why I was aghast this morning when the yoga teacher looked at me during advanced side plank pose and from clear across the room boomed, "You don't trust yourself." Just blurted it out for the entire world to hear, like a dinner guest would drop a political bomb on the table while the appetizers were being passed.

Her words hit so hard I exhaled audibly. It was that *knowing* that somebody has seen right through your charade, that painful truth that smacks with a *gotcha*. I felt what she said in my bones, where

Bidden

or not bidden,

God is present.

✢ *16th century monk Desiderius Eramus*

the truth of what she said laid hiding, concealed like a secret in my storehouse of doubt. Moreover—or so it seemed in that moment—she broke the rules of etiquette and the usual niceties afforded a studio visitor. How dare she?

And besides, how could she see my distrust from ten feet away? I mean, she didn't actually *know* me; I just happened to walk into her studio and unroll my mat, trying to squeeze in a little mid-tour yoga. I felt like announcing to the whole class, OK! *Alright already! I have trust issues! With God, with myself, with my life. Now can we all just get back to our mats and do a little stretching together please?*

I didn't, of course. I'm way too courteous, honed by years and years of perfect dinner party etiquette.

I did what I usually do when un-pleasantries are hurled in my direction, justified or not: I suffered. Like eating a dinner entrée I don't really like, I swallowed it whole and pretended everything was fine, too insecure to admit, even to myself, that I didn't like how it tasted.

Life lessons aren't always served up on a silver platter. It also seems the more you ignore the truth, the more it tries to grab your attention. There are no kittens in the room, after all—only elephants. And God and Truth—well, they exist on the same planet, and I often see them as synonymous. "Bidden or not bidden, God is present," said the 16th century monk Desiderius Eramus. Meaning, the Divine, the truth, is always present, whether you believe it or not. Today it showed up in advanced side plank pose, tapped me on my uncertain shoulder, and said, *Now, can we please deal with pretending you host faith? Clearly you don't. You can't even shoulder the weight of your own body.*

This is confusing, to say the least. I can glide into full splits on the ground, in a pose known as Hanumanasana, with the greatest of ease. My hamstrings are dependable. They feel at home on earth. The pose is named after the monkey god who leaped over the ocean to an island, to rescue Sita, the beloved of Rama, to whom Hanuman was wholly devoted. Hanuman took one look at the span he had to cross, thinking something along the lines of, "there's no way in hell I can do that," and then took a leap anyway. Who hasn't thought the same thing when faced with a colossal challenge? Who hasn't faltered and walked away, thinking, *god no, I can't do that, are you kidding me?*

Yoga poses, of course, are microcosms for other aspects of our life. When I move into an advanced version of side plank pose, my lower leg crumbles at the knee as I lift my upper leg. My fingers fumble as they try to find my big toe in the air. Meanwhile, my shoulder trembles in fear and I lose the connection with my hand on the ground. I can pull it off, sure, but it was that teacher who saw what's always troubled me about the pose: The way I waver.

I suspect part of my trepidation in finding the full expression of this arm balance is derived from all those dinner parties, where it was considered gauche to place my elbows on the table. I'm afraid to let these little joints that connect my upper and lower arm hold me steady and strong. These dainty feminine joints are eternally genteel, hidden, discouraged from showing their power.

In other words, I can't depend on my own hands. Which is ridiculous, really. These are, after all, the same hands that have effortlessly cleared bowls of vichyssoise soup moments before the main course, served dessert perfectly timed with fresh-brewed coffee, and hand-washed my grandmother's wedding china at 2am after serving a seven-course meal to 20 people. They're the same hands that planted English roses for David's birthday, held my best friend's hand when he was dying of cancer, and were raised up in the air to confess that I, too, am an alcoholic. Where's the trust? Arm balances speak for me when I can't admit my own insecurities. They also take me to places I'd prefer to overlook. That's the beauty and curse of yoga: It's unpeeling one layer to find another, and cultivating the resilience to keep truckin'.

Rather than buying into the hype "have faith" or the ubiquitous "it's all good," I found it healing, after that class, to slow down and spend some time in the hurt that teacher evoked, even in the darker places of worry and distress. These energies have a weightiness to them, like straps that keep hot air balloons from floating off into the ether. They beg to break through, to become transformed into higher action. Maybe hanging out in side plank can show me it's not my shoulder that's weak, or that my connection to my heart and the earth that's unsteady. It's my outer hamstring that's unsure.

Formally known as the biceps femoris, it's the part of the leg that makes taking a big step forward possible. It's the largest contributor to hip extension. It's also one of the most difficult muscles to strengthen and have confidence in.

And so is my relationship with faith. I've had to build it. In Sanskrit, the word for faith is *shraddha*. It's not blind faith; it's faith based on experience. We all have doubt and we all have fear—they never really go away—but we can become more skillful at managing them. Advanced side plank pose is challenging and complex. That teacher was right: It brings up every bit of self-doubt I have—about the pose, yes, but also about the tour and love and life decisions. The pose matches how I feel most days: overwhelmed. I recognize the edginess of my relationship with my obliques, that wondering if there's mutual support, as the same feeling that emerges on show day, when weirdness hangs in the air between David and me. We're under tight schedules and in close quarters; there are short fuses all around. And just like I want to collapse in side plank, I lose faith in walking the path on which I've found myself. What has happened to my life? Have I made a mistake, thinking I could survive out here on the road without fresh air, close friends, and my own rituals of proper living? How have I found myself in a life where fragile porcelain is the very last thing of consequence?

Journey's timeless classic, "Don't Stop Believin'," is about believing in yourself so much that ordinary appearances or current life circumstances don't distract or distress you from living in harmony with your heart. It's not dogmatic faith. It's not a worship of Hanuman or any deity Out There. It's a bow to the internal energy of self-trust. On one hand, this tour life looks as far away from a yogic lifestyle and a southern girl's existence as humanly possible. Yet on the other hand, it's very clear that it is all about yoga.

Audubon once said, "When the book and the bird disagree, believe the bird." This entire tour, and not just an arm balance, is an exercise in faith. The fans will show up, I tell myself. David will be healthy and excited and able to perform well, and he—the David I love, not the Dave on stage—will return to me with time. I *will* find a salad bar that carries more than iceberg. The sixth chapter of the *Bhagavad Gita* poses the possibility of "seeing the unseeable" and "hearing the unhearable," which, like this tour, doesn't make any sense at first. Then you find yourself in a world so foreign that faith is the only thing that *does* make sense. "Faith is not a belief," Ram Dass said. "Faith is what is left when all your beliefs have been blown to hell."

Once upon a time my biggest concerns were how to make a dinner table inviting and how to match the perfect wine with the main dish. In my new job I host hundreds of people at over 100 concerts per year. In both cases I want the guests to feel full and nourished and loved; well-fed and taken care of. Now, I'm just working on a bigger scale and without the fine china. I've had to learn not only how to make our guests feel welcome, but also how to receive all the complexities of a life lived in perpetual forward motion.

Simply worshipping a higher power, be it Hanuman, Allah, Buddha, or The Beatles, can't possibly hold the immensity of genuine trust. Faith doesn't point a finger to the sky but surrenders to a deep amen within. "Hold on to that feeling," the song says, and yogis would agree. Faith and self-confidence are dance partners.

At the show tonight, standing in the back of the concert hall on floors so hard the arches of my feet ached in my Stuart Weitzman 5050 boots, I could feel the first stirrings of skepticism. It had been a busy merch night so far, and I'd run back to the bus twice to restock vinyl albums. On the last trip I grabbed an extra stock; I had a hunch it was going to be gangbusters after the show.

This was a wine crowd, and my thoughts returned to the woman who threw wine at her husband at that dinner party so many years ago. There was no wine-throwing going on at the concert, but it wouldn't have been surprising, given the fact that it was the world of anything-goes-rock-and-roll. But it occurred to me as I stood there, anticipating my own showtime and calming my inner voices, that it takes real guts—more than inebriation—to have the kind of self-confidence to toss a full glass of red at a fancy dinner table. It's the kind of assurance that I found three years ago when I quit eating meat and took a pass on the pork roast at a Sunday dinner. "Are you a vegetarian?" people asked with the same raised eyebrows I see when I turn my wine glass upside down to indicate I won't be drinking. "Is that a yoga thing or is there something wrong with you?" a hostess once asked me. I could have unloaded a whole platter of sticky yams right on top of her.

I didn't, though—not so much because I'm well-versed in table manners but because yoga is teaching me I have other choices. Making a point to a mere acquaintance is one thing. Making a glacial internal shift is another thing entirely. I've learned to stop defending my table choices and just eat my carrots and broccoli in peace. This is the definition of wisely conserving my energy.

But that yoga teacher from this morning? That's a different story. She was haunting me. Because she was right; she'd called out the elephant in the room. While mineral water and veggies can fill you up for dinner, I struggle with what Buddhists describe as "hungry ghost" syndrome. Classically portrayed as figures with little necks and huge bellies, these ghouls signify our inability to satisfy our powerful, earthly desires. Our basic sense of self-worth is unmet, no matter how many high-end boots we splurge on or arm balances we nail. We keep searching for it, as tirelessly as a spirit stuck between here and heaven; we hunt for satiation in alcohol and approval; in place settings and plank pose. "Working hard to get our fill. Everybody wants a thrill," because we don't believe our lives exactly as they are, are thrilling enough.

Einstein once remarked, "The most important decision we make is whether we believe we live in a friendly or hostile universe." The *asana* practices of yoga are here to help create ease and to touch the real—a concept based not on made-up rules of etiquette but on *shraddha*. We align our bodies with confidence, and by extension we have the same strength in the world, which is why this morning caught me off guard. It triggered the fact that I'm prowling this planet without the self-acceptance and self-trust I crave. I'm looking and looking and looking, and hoping my timeliness in attending classes, my devotion to the practice, my just-laundered Lululemons (a miracle on tour) will shroud this. That teacher's words stunned me because I can pretend to others—myself included—that I've come so far. That, by virtue of identifying as a yogi, I have unshakable self-faith.

Hardly. But I do have the ability to observe, process, and learn. That teacher had something to teach me, and it went way beyond the pose. She was honest and brave enough to speak the truth. And if I can make that jump of perception, I can also consider learning how to put these God-given hamstrings to new use and do advanced side plank for real. And perhaps, even, begin to exorcise those hungry ghosts by feeding them faith instead of indulging them with *you need this and that and that and this to ever feel full.*

Fear and worry thrive, as the song puts it, by "living in a lonely world," and in my book, there's nothing lonelier than a ghost lingering between two worlds. Faith, on the other hand, resides in connection, to hamstrings asked to work harder than they're used to, to nodding towards those hungry ghosts who howl during a 30-day tour, and to hearing hard truths when you think you've succeeded. We can begin to trust in a world, not of ideas, but of firsthand experience. To no longer be "strangers, waitin', up and down the boulevard, their shadows searchin' in the night," as the song says, but to be present in our own bodies and resolute in our own hearts, for both the ups and the downs that inevitably happen in life, because we are nurtured from within. Undaunted when a spoon is out of place on a table, or when a road forks into unseen territory.

I didn't sell all five boxes of albums at the merch table that night, but I was prepared all the same. I did, however, write a yoga class in a quiet corner of the bus in the wee hours of the night, a course sequenced with advanced side plank pose and Hanumanasana. When I was done, I practiced it in silence. Once I became aware that my trusty hamstrings could drive the pose, advanced side plank was easy. It's just Hanumanasana turned on her side.

This fed my hungry soul. It satisfied my whole being. This was one of the first nights in a long time my disbelieving, internal voices were at rest. I invested time in something I trusted in, that nourished me and also spoke to taking a big leap in self-care. I wanted to record the solid data of that *head-to-toe feeling* so that when I heard the distant echo of "you don't trust yourself" again I'd be prepared. My table would be set. And I'd answer back, "Yeah really? Not biting."

Compassion

Trikonasana
Extended Triangle Pose

7

While My Guitar Gently Weeps

The yoga sutras don't have a whole lot to say about where to place your hands or your feet but they do offer plenty of instruction on where to place your heart. The *yamas* and *niyamas*, sutra 1.33, and other astute suggestions help us keep our hearts in the right spot. The energetic heart center, what yogis call the *anahata*, translates as "not broken." It evokes a sweeter, kinder truth: that we don't need to make our hearts bigger or better. Rather, we could use a good clearing.

I'm not sure if yoga is more healing during a pose or after; if the magic potion is found in experiencing the aches in a posture or in the rush of relief when I release it. But I do know that where and how I spend my time after a tour feels more nourishing than being out on the road, no matter how fabulous the itinerary promises.

As soon as I come home to Maui, I throw on my bikini before the bags have been unpacked and dash down the street to Keawakapu Beach. I plant myself, face to the sun, on the sand. No hat, no sunscreen, no shame in my 58-year-old body. Nothing can stop me from the utter enjoyment of soaking in the warmth of each grain of sand. I feel the millions of them welcoming me back to the island, and even more, back to myself. The sound of the ocean, the sway of the palms, the smell of salty air—this ritual of returning is pure heaven. My mood when I'm on Maui doesn't fall far from the coconut tree. Island life appeals to me.

On this particular reunion, I feel so light and happy I practically skip down the street on my way home from the beach. The colors are luminous; flowers are everywhere. I quicken my pace the closer I get to the front door. I round the corner and see our plumeria, so packed with blossoms I smell the tree before I see it. But no sooner do I open the door than David proclaims, "I'm gonna sell this place."

David and I couldn't be on two more opposite sides of the

universe regarding this matter, and listening to him pronounce such blasphemy sends me into orbit. I can hardly feel my feet on the ground, let alone focus.

    This disorientation lasts for a week, even after trying to find my heart, my center, with daily yoga classes and afternoon swims in the ocean. I can't shake the steady, low-grade panic that emerges at the mere mention of selling our house in Hawaii.

    He does this, David—these vast decrees, these commandments on high—and he performs them with such skillful mastery you almost believe them to be fact. It's how we ended up married. One day he just announced, "Well, I guess it's time we got married," like there wasn't another person involved in the decision. "I hope that's not your idea of a proposal," I replied, which set off a five-year showdown on the subject simply because I wanted to have a say in the matter and to be asked nicely. This Hawaii house thing is just like that. "I hope this isn't your idea of where we will be living," he says one morning. Oh. My. God. I mean, *really?*

    Of course it's a bigger issue than just selling a house. It's jettisoning a lifestyle; it's bulldozing my dream. Hawaii is beauty and beaches, to be sure, but she's much more than that too. She's a land of lessons, and like any great beauty, she comes with innumerable complexities; fire and instabilities. Her islands were formed by volcanic activity over a hot spot in the planet's mantle. Occasionally she erupts and gets cracked open. Her insides spill out, simultaneously destroying old paths and creating new ones. Islands grow and evolve; her landscape is forever changed. This magnificent transformation happens from incredible depths, and in one of the most remote locations in the world.

    This is my third go-around of trying to live in Hawaii, in this lifetime at least. I'm sure we've been at this, Hawaii and me, way longer. This time I've landed in South Maui, in a lovely, modest bungalow. No pool, no view, nothing fancy, which is a huge part of the place's charm. Architecturally the house is very 60s, even though it was built in the 70s, when Wailea was little more than cacti and kiawes. This naturally wild land has been tamed, and around its lushness rests some of the most stunning beaches in the state. Our unfussy neighborhood is now surrounded by some of the poshest homes in Hawaii. And, like Hawaii's contrasts and contradictions, my path here never has been straightforward. It continually requires adjustments and fine tuning.

I never just accidentally arrive in Hawaii, either; it's a calling, she's an invitation, and like these hauntingly bewitching islands themselves, my experience here has been fierce and complicated. Always alongside me is a battle of belonging and self-worth, an ancient yearning for connection in an ever-changing world.

These musings show up here more than any other place. Or maybe they're always lurking, but I'm willing to be more vulnerable on Maui; more open and available to face myself. When I fall apart on the island, I'm caught, always, in the gentle, loving rock of her ocean waves and the majesty of her breathtaking sunsets. Almost every evening I watch the day turn to night from my perch on the sand. It's reassurance, mainly—that even as the sky turns dark it's never without light. The stars and the moonbeams walk home with me, my heart turned to the sky. Hawaii is my spiritual home and I love her like no place on Earth.

Life in Hawaii, not as a tourist, but as a yogini, is extra interesting. I guess that's what you call it when your heart explodes in yoga class. Mine got cracked wide open, mid-air, as I was rising into trikonasana, or triangle pose, in a morning vinyasa class, only a few weeks after David's brute pronouncement regarding the fate of our darling house. Pain hit my chest with such intense burning it brought me to my knees. Heartache does that. It's the worst brand of sting, especially when it sneaks up on you.

What I was attempting to practice, more than trikonasana, was a state of mind yogis call *karuna*. Usually translated as compassion and linked to forgiveness, it's one of Buddhism's four immeasurables and one of Patanjali's first suggestions on how we might connect to ourselves and others.

Neither compassion nor forgiveness are my strong suits. I can be hard in that way, and it's a terrible burden to bear the world without these qualities. I have a habit of holding people at arm's length so that their behavior can never really bother me; so that I don't have to tap into wells of compassion and forgiveness for their misdemeanors of character.

But I can't do that with David, bless his soul; we're in too deep. And this argument has me furious with him for even suggesting we sell Maui. I can barely stand to be in this house I love so much with a man who's *so hateful*. How can he possibly not see the value of our home, literally and spiritually? How dare he not value me and how I feel about it? Can he not see me? *Does* he not see me?

Like some alignments of the heart that don't make it to the surface of our lives—at least with any grace and ease—some lines in music don't make it to the song. There's a rumor George (I call him George because he's my other rock-and-roll husband, and I usually write, under a degree of protest from David, with his photo in a little silver frame on my desk) wrote:

The problems you sow, are the troubles you're reaping,
Still, my guitar gently weeps

Legend says this song has its roots in the I Ching, the Chinese Book of Changes, deeply beloved by truth seekers and soul journeymen because, if you haven't noticed, things are changing all the time, including us. George wrote "While My Guitar Gently Weeps" at his mother's house in Warrington, England, later declaring, "The Eastern concept is that whatever happens is all meant to be, and that there's no such thing as coincidence—every little item that's going down has a purpose."

Both George's song and the practice of compassion have roots in the yogic notion of karma, which goes something like:

As I am, so I act;
As I act, so I become

The key to karma and true transformation, as pointed out by Ravi Ravindra, is in the semicolon. There's a dot to make us stop and a comma to encourage a pause. The prescription for pain is not so much self-improvement; it's self-study. "Yesterday I was clever, so I wanted to change the world. Today I am wise, so I am changing myself," Rumi said. Direct observation of how you act is required for any deep, lasting change. You have to see what's holding you tight in order to loosen your death grip on joy. It's in the space to notice; to clearly see how you're acting and own it, because you are the sum of your actions. It's a crossing over of the threshold of self-love by embracing both the pleasant and unpleasant aspects of what you see. This calls for a marvelous capacity for compassion.

The law of karma is often bemoaned as if the dye of our lives is cast. But, as Ravindra points out, the law of karma is actually the law of freedom. I feel imprisoned by David's whims but I'm also letting it catapult a shift in perception. When you see how you are acting, after all, you have options. You can choose to continue your behavior, or you can change. If you change how you act, you'll change who you become. And if you change who you are you will change your life. Self-empowerment is almost always available. Change is a choice. So is blame, disappointment, and feeling sorry for yourself.

Just as a guitar was George's instrument, our hearts are ours. Can we operate from a place of forgiveness and compassion? Can we offer our kinder selves to others; can we embody what George says when he sings, "I look at you all and see the love there that's sleeping?"

Everybody has their favorite Beatle, and George is my favorite not only because he's the cutest but also because he wrote such insightful lyrics. Does anything get better than "with every mistake we must surely be learning?" Not to my ears. Humming this line helps land compassion in my heart. I'm learning something from this, I tell myself, and this alone is enlivening.

Compassion, like trikonasana, activates the whole body. It takes everything you have to meet yourself as well as see each other with love. It finds the balance between being rooted in the lower body, strong like a warrior, and present and open to the real, so that the upper body can extend long and free and the heart can turn to higher ground. Trikonasana translates as "triangle" or "three angle asana," and triangles themselves are often linked to trinities. In Christianity, it's the Father, the Son, and the Holy Ghost. In

Hinduism, it's the Trimurti of Brahman, Vishnu, and Shiva. The triangle can also symbolize the stages of the moon: waxing, waning, and full. Other trinities are mind, body, and spirit, or mother, father, and child, or past, present, and future. It's multi-sided, and the practice of her—of both compassion and trikonasana—helps us feel our wholeness.

Having a panic attack in yoga was a big semicolon. It stopped me from transitioning to a standing pose just like this house situation is holding me back from taking a stand in my own power. And maybe that's the purpose of the synchronicity of all the messiness surrounding the house and the pose and my heart and my husband stopping me from rising up to take the bait of hopelessness and anger. There was a pause, a moment to become fully present, which is where truth typically reveals herself. There was no weeping or poor-me wallowing. It was a battle cry for a fresh perspective, perhaps a new trinity. Not 'his' way, not 'my' way, but 'our' way. We're married, for goodness sake (and yes, I finally got a say in it).

After the initial hit to my heart in class, I realized this: I cannot be a victim to the traditional ties of marriage, or of the mind. Who says the man is always the breadwinner? Who says the man makes all the choices? Who says whether Hawaii is a good investment or one whose time is up? I was already on my knees, having been forced there by a hurt heart, and so I asked for help. I asked for clarity and strength, and for guidance to ease my pain. I asked for compassion for me and for David. I included our dog Star, our sweet little bungalow, and the entire island of Maui in my prayers. The Dalai Lama says, "If you want others to be happy, practice compassion. If you want to be happy, practice compassion." And if nothing else, I excel at practicing.

But *karuna* was hard work, I have to say. I was holding on to this anger and I was mad at David. I was mad at men, all of them, as a whole tribe. (Ouch, how painful.) But I was mainly mad at myself and my long history of giving away my power, partly in the name of co-dependence, and partly for adhering to the old-fashioned belief, passed down through generations, that a woman's place is behind her man. This inborn thought exists in me so casually, like I inherited a hand-knitted sweater or something.

And yet, the practice of *karuna*, as dysregulating as it was, helped me slacken my grip on the rage I felt—enough where I could see that I have a choice in this matter. I could be silent and invisible and seething like my old patterns of relationship, or I could forgive myself simply because my bank account is lower than David's. I'm the one who left my career to tour with him. It was one of the best choices I've ever made, but like the shifting tectonic plates deep below these islands, I can and must shift my own heartstrings in order for it to continue working. If I don't value my own art, how can I expect David to take me seriously when I carry on about my dreams and don't follow through with the same intensity as I tour? I mean, I can do both. I juggle a thousand jobs out on tour; why not slide one in for myself? Why not find that third side to a triangle that balances out the other two?

Still, I was stuck and confused about what it means to be a wife. What is the duty of relationship and what is the obligation to nurturing one's deepest self? I might not have had a heart attack in the classic sense, but these questions attacked my heart with such a ferocious smack it knocked me off my own capable legs. I thought: *Who am I fighting more, the institution of marriage, David or myself?* Which was quickly followed by *Oh my God, I'm a mess. Who would ever take a yoga class from me? Who would ever listen to me tell them how to put the sole of their foot below their knee or their soul in alignment with their heart?*

Hogwash, I say now. The greatest warriors I know, who happen to be women by the way, don't present themselves as perfect and pretend to have it all together. Their power and wisdom comes from broken hearts and hard-won battles with anxiety, depression, relationships, addiction, money, sex—you name it. They have learned to forgive themselves. They have dropped their anger and blame against others. They've taken a stand in their own command. Maybe I'm starting to be more real, more believable, precisely because I struggle.

In the end, I practiced forgiveness and compassion for myself that morning on my mat in a new, more authentic way. It felt awkward and scary and it made my heart beat with even more intensity. I wobbled up and finished the other side of the standing sequence, and as I transitioned from warrior into my second-go at trikonasana, I chose a roomier version where my hand was on my shin and my gaze fell to the floor. My legs were solid and straight; my heart, though, surrendered to the fight. "The gap between compassion and surrender is love's darkest, deepest region," says Turkish Nobel laureate Orhan Pamuk. He is right. I returned to the ground and twisted. And I laid in savasana in pain and fear, gasping for air because I thought it could be my last.

Yoga, once again, knocked the wind right out of me. But I got up. I rolled up my mat and got into my car and offered my heart up, literally, for examination. I went to Urgent Care after class.

My EKG report indicated that my heart was strong. My blood test confirmed I was well-hydrated and clean. I'd like to think, now, that this volcanic eruption of my heart cleansed a path of destructive thinking about relationships and roles, about dignity and belonging, about forgiveness and freedom. Part of my heart changed as a result of refusing to breathe the toxic fumes of low self-esteem and self-worth. Of anger and worry and fear.

Now, from time to time, this anxiety still happens. I panic, and I struggle. And then I break free to make it to the other side, a little bit stronger, a little bit sweeter to myself. My angst is not as severe as it once was, and I figure this is a symptom of healing that I can track directly to the practice of forgiveness and compassion. A practice of willing to have my heart looked at not only by myself, but trust others to help me check myself, including a nice team of doctors. Even though it felt silly and humbling to be told that I was fine and all was well. Even though it cost $600 and a full afternoon of tests.

Well, maybe the trip to Urgent Care was a little embarrassing, perhaps melodramatic. But it gave texture to forgiveness and compassion. It gave me *something to work on*.

Ultimately, I see, compassion has a way of softening the edges of your heart the same way Hawaii's jagged lava transforms into the finest of sands and the most beautiful of beaches. It takes time. It takes unwavering patience and steadfast trust. I sort of, almost, maybe, began to breathe a little better after that attempt at *karuna*. I was easier on myself more than usual. I took a lot of long beach walks and frequent naps, and backed off of difficult yoga poses and heated encounters with David.

I also began to see that I'm exhausted from the last tour and could consider, with compassion, the fact that David has been doing it for *50 years*. I can see how cashing it all in and kicking back a little more might be desirable, and if this means selling our Maui home then I've got to at least try to understand it. And while David has made some bad choices that have put him in the crosshairs of working and retirement, I can also see I've made my own terrible choices too. (Who hasn't?) Meanwhile I'm smack in the middle of one by being angry with him for my own decisions, which have left me without enough cash to just buy the Maui house on my own. Compassion, however, holds you like a sun-warmed beach when you accept the consequences, and beauties, of being who you are.

A month passed on Maui and the days of leisure melted towards the beginning of another tour. A week before we were due to hit the road I overheard David on the phone. "What time can you be here tomorrow?" I assumed it was tour-related but when he hung up he announced, "We're building a pool."

I didn't know what was more shocking: his change of heart regarding the house or his use of the coveted "we." Not that I had any say in the pool matter decision, but it was a huge step in the direction towards us-ness.

I venture to say the future of our little Maui house will be an ongoing discussion. Hawaii never disappoints in that way. Now, though? I have new tools to deal with the heat.

Wonder

Eka Pada Urdhva Dhanurasana
One-Legged Wheel Pose

8
School's Out

Growing up, I was spoon-fed the belief that smart means secure. There was no room to wonder if college was the right choice or if your career would "make you happy." It was all planned out, well in advance, by high school counselors, university advisors, my parents, and the evening news; it scarcely had anything to do with my heart's calling. A college degree, I was taught, was a tacit guarantee that my professional and personal life would unfold without a hitch. Education was a life essential, right alongside scoring a desk job, getting married, and having children—the latter two overshadowing the first in terms of importance. The entire thing was an outsider's set-up for a life that didn't look like anything I'd enjoy living. But I completed them all—minus the kids—because it was what people I knew did. They looked happy enough.

I also did them because I knew it was crucial to gaining my parents' approval and to ensuring—or at least trying to ensure—my security in the world. I not only got a Bachelor's degree but also a Master's, as well as a thousand and one workshop and specialty degrees. There was seldom a time I *wasn't* in school, or enrolled in some sort of specialized training. Answers to life's questions, I thought, existed outside of myself, and I was hell-bent on finding them. My parents cheered it all on from the sidelines.

But the more degrees I got, the more bewildered I became. Living as a stick-to-the-books kind of girl eventually got me in a lot of trouble because I wasn't aware of whose knowledge I had absorbed or whose values I'd bought. The customer isn't always right, carbs are not the enemy, lightning *does* strike twice, and wearing horizontal stripes won't make you look bigger. The Upanishads say, "Into blind darkness they enter those who worship ignorance. Into still greater darkness enter those who worship knowledge." I discovered that, while being a lifelong learner, whatever that might look like, is

Keep your face

toward the sunshine

and the shadows

will fall behind you.

✦ Walt Whitman

as imperative as kindness and curiosity, the *need to know* in order to feel secure and worthy and loved will keep you enrolled in school for a very, very long time. The real stuff—self-love, trust in the universe, and authenticity—aren't taught in books.

Neither is God, in the truest, more irrefutable sense, which often leaves me thinking of Julian Barnes, who once said, "I don't believe in God, but I miss him." The thing is, I *do* believe in God, he or she or it being a grand universal consciousness. Sometimes, though, I want God to appear in black and white on the page, just as I want confirmation that life will turn out well and that David will always cherish me.

The fact that I can't find answers to these questions in books or a blog post has left me suspect, doubting everything. I want things to play out as I think they should; I want God to assure me of his existence. When I wonder what I'm doing out on tour, this unplanned, radical departure from what I and my parents thought I would be doing with my life, I feel that my prayers to the universe to give me a sign—my plea with the heavens to send me comfort—go unanswered. I toss and turn at night, my ears specially tuned to every sound that might emerge. I agonize and distress and pray some more and worry that it feels like too static of an effort. So I get up beside David and open the slats of the bus shades and look at the moon and ask the stars, *Am I doing it right?* The answer to this seems critical. Very little of my education has prepared me for marriage to a musician, or rock-and-roll touring, or love or death or existential crises. (My 8th grade Spanish class did come in handy last week, though, when we played in Puerto Vallarta.)

What I do know is that I can let my emotions drive me clear out of my body. It's incredibly uncomfortable, for me and everyone in my orbit, especially in the midst of touring when all-too-close proximity to other people is relentless. When the machine is in full whirl, the tour bus feels more like a rocket ship. I forget basic life skills like taking a big deep breath, or smiling.

In an effort to find some sure footing on the road, I've had to explore new ways of relating to this planet I inhabit. But instead of looking down—of literally standing over what I think I know, like my own two feet—I've decided to start looking up. Why? Because this immense new world isn't just underfoot, it's all around me. And, like love and God, it's all *way over my head.*

Hafiz wrote, "Let's stop reading about God. We will never understand him. Jump to your feet, wave your fists, threaten and warn the whole universe that your heart can no longer live without real love." I did just that, tonight, on this late summer evening in New Hampshire. Well, I wasn't as eloquent as Hafiz, since a howl accompanied it, but the jumping and fist-waving were spot on.

I'd ducked out the fire exit of the concert venue where David was playing and into an adjoining empty field, certain nobody could see me. It was just me and a blanket of stars and my loud-as-all-get-out wail that boomed into the universe before it was swallowed up by the dark, glittering sky. The silence that followed left me standing stock still; there wasn't even an echo. Chagrined, I was about to drop my head and trudge back to the show when I saw the sweetest, tiny sliver of moon slip from behind a cloud and come into full view. We looked at each other for what seemed a long while, as if it had heard my call.

I'd seen the moon before, of course, but this evening it struck me that it was something I actually knew very little about. The night sky enraptured me so completely it melted any semblance of a cool façade, any claim that I could figure life out, any rights to Smarty-Pants-Ville. I was fooling exactly no one, anyway, of course. And besides that, is there anything more boorish than a know-it-all?

"Really," a friend once said to me, "if you ever think you know everything about everything, just look up into the sky." Try to wrap your mind around the fact that by staring at a star you're peering into the past. Attempt to know, genuinely know, that if something hit the brightest star in the sky—our Sirius—we wouldn't see it happen for nearly a decade. Imagine all that we cannot fathom about space and galaxies and see if what you learned in school makes you as intelligent as you might believe yourself to be—the "you" here, of course, being me.

My love affair with the moon and stars didn't start tonight, nor did it begin by asking permission. It didn't start by consulting astrologers or reading books. It was raw and organic; pure wonder and awe. And it has left me thinking a lot about what I don't know about this life, and of the love that's rumored to right it.

Dante wrote about "the love that moves the sun and the other stars," which sounds like science fiction until we ourselves experience the emotion of unconditional love, whether it arrives from the Divine or the person we share a bed with. Love may be the most challenging thing to do, but it's the most ubiquitous of alignments in all wisdom traditions. The practices of yoga help us see the ways we hold our minds small, our bodies tight, our hearts hardened, ourselves resistant to the love that might just be in our ambit. As we relax into a posture and into a life, we have the possibility to see its possibility in new, wondrous ways.

Or so they say—and so I'd like to think. I mean, it all sounds so lovely and sparkly and forever-ish, doesn't it? But who has time to moon over this on a rock-and-roll tour? The precision with which details must be attended to, from the location of the stage door to the time of the venue's curfew, can make or break a whole show, or, in my case, a marriage. The *need to know* so much information day in and day out, every day, for weeks on end, makes the one with all the answers the real star of the show.

The truth, that sweet little sliver of a moon showed me tonight, is that we never really know much about anything—and there's a universe of growth and opportunity within this. It's not the unknown but what we *think* we know that undoes us. I think I know what yoga teachers are supposed to look like—social media reminds me of this daily—and it contaminates my capacity to love my (very able) body. I know failed relationships, and this taints how I view the present with David and how I operate within our marriage. I worry about ruining another "perfectly good" relationship with my suffering because what I'm learning more and more in the middle of Godknowswhere, in some hotel parking lot at 3am, in a comfy Prevost bus, is that I am out on tour mainly to gain my husband's affection. In the name of Dante's proclamation of what love should *be*.

This is all on me, you see. David is plenty generous with his pleases and thank yous, his compliments and I love yous, his *this tour would be harder without yous*. But this uncertainty I feel between us at times, this thrumming nervousness inside of me, feels like it will never be complete; that the destination, the finality of its answers, can never be reached. It's not like knowing a Shakespeare love sonnet by rote, or the latest General Accepted Accounting Principle regarding depreciation of an asset. There's a mysterious quality to our connection, mine and David's and mine and God's, the depths of which I'll never comprehend. Sometimes this is enticing, and as magical as it sounds. Other times it's maddening in its elusiveness. You can't pinpoint anything permanent or unequivocally certain about the presences of these entities I worship; you can't say for sure what tomorrow will carry. And I want that, once in a while. The stability of something sound and immovable and there, *there*, always.

Am I forgetting that such permanence is all Hollywood fiction? Have I seen too many romantic comedies? Because tonight, before I fled through the fire exit, it didn't feel so funny.

The life of a yogi and of a touring rock-and-roller haunts me, in part because it makes me feel like a rebel, and I was never one to go against the grain. I spent most of my life trying to fit in; I was groomed to color within the lines. Perfection and meeting others' expectations long ruled my existence. At my age, I should be shuttling kids into college, driving a white SUV, getting weekly blowouts, baking bread, maybe tending a garden. So when I caught myself howling at the moon just a few hours ago, with my unwashed hair and backless dress, I was pretty sure I'd lost it. Yet, the moon was so beautiful, and so were the twinkling stars. I thought *why not?* I've always wondered what a little yelp would feel like.

It was so fun.

And maybe I'm not lost at all. Maybe I'm just finding myself.

For me, Alice Cooper's "School's Out" isn't a call to rebellion in the classic sense. Rather, it's an anthem of freedom, which is precisely what happens when you unleash yourself from the conditioning

It is only with the heart that one sees rightly. What is essential is invisible to the eye.

※ *Antoine de Saint-Exupery*

of your roles, your identity, your regular ways of being. Touring is about as far away from a desk job as it gets. I don't think my parents had a rock legend fifteen years my senior in mind when they advocated I get married. Nor do I think most of society would agree with me when I think of our audience members as family David and I are nurturing through harmonies. Even the life of a yogi, in this modern, trendy era, is outside of my grasp. Slick magazine covers portray "star" yogis with beautiful bodies. Yoga conferences pack mat-to-mat rooms with "master" teachers. IG showcases yoginis in Alo clothes, their figures rivaling the girls over at Victoria's Secret. Inherently, there's nothing sinister about any of this (although there is cause for concern over the sexualization in yoga), but, quite honestly, it leaves out the majority of us. Loud music, meanwhile, doesn't exactly engender the quiet mind most yogis talk about, or conjure a woman who is 58. And yet, here I am, with a mostly stable job and a mostly steady mind, on my way towards realizing that home really is where your heart is. And I got here not because I followed a traditional track but because I let myself wonder, and then allowed my feet to follow where that wondering wanted to go.

Leaning into wonder and the unknown doesn't mean becoming ignorant. It means unlocking yourself to possibilities as infinite as the night sky seems, to me, to be. It celebrates the enigmatic, hidden dimensions in people and situations that extend beyond what we can view and touch and understand immediately. Wonder means keeping your mind and heart open for surprises. Stopping for biscuits and gravy at a Cracker Barrel is about as un-rock star as it gets, and yet the recollection of this still strikes me as one of the highlights of our most recent tour. Cooper writes, "No more pencils, no more books, no more teacher's dirty looks," and I'm coming to share these feelings when it comes to conforming to what the life a woman of my age looks like, or how a yogi should appear. It also makes me wonder—about wrong turns and right turns and what, really, this all means.

"Wonder is the foundation of yoga," it says in the Shiva Sutras, and so I try to remind myself of this. I have no concrete proof of God, or that my relationship with David is my manifestation of Dante's theory. But I have seen wonder in the middle of the night when I can't sleep and my little white Maltese crawls on my chest and stays there until I doze back off. I've lived wonder as I've rolled down the highway looking at my 73-year-old—this man who has spent his life on the road—and contemplated the amount of sacrifice he's given for his art. I've looked down at my feet and felt wonder as I contemplated how in the world did my buttoned-up, smart girl self end up in a place that often sounds like madness and smells like pot smoke. Wonder, I'm seeing, is the foundation because yoga meets you where you are and not a second before. It reminds us that all of our schooling, all of our experience, should be shed the moment we step on our mats. It tells us to approach each pose, no matter how many times we've done it, as if it's brand new. It urges us to do the same with love, and every other life endeavor, no matter how big or small.

We all want to know what happens next in life, and that's the bazillion dollar question. Yoga says that what happens next is coming right on schedule. The best we can do for our future is be present *right now*. Yoga also says the answers to what we really need to know reside, quietly, inside.

Asana does this, keeping our bodies and minds supple enough to embrace wonder, while simultaneously reminding us that we have "felt wisdom" as old as stars within us. Eka pada urhavadhanurasana— or One-Legged Wheel Pose—is just one pose that gets us closer to this truth. While there are many little postures that build up to this complex pose, what it can offer for all bodies, on a soul level, is a play in the energies of turning things upside down, where true freedom of mind dwells. It holds us still while our point of view shifts from the known into something you can't see but can most definitely feel. It requires being comfortable with opening your heart in the biggest and most vulnerable of ways, and finding balance even though the whole picture isn't in view. Your *I can't even see what my legs are doing, school's* definitely *out*, and wonder is keeping the whole shape afloat.

In such a deep backbend, the low, floating ribs must temper

It is the lack of love that makes everything stale, dull and uninteresting.

✦ *Ravi Ravindra*

themselves towards the navel so that the kidneys have some breathing room. The naval center is said to be our sun, but the truth is everybody has their own anatomical center. Regardless of where it rests, you can't learn how to hold your heart open even if Iyengar himself said it to you, just as you can't learn God from schoolbooks, or love from rom-coms. You have to learn to feel it, from the inside. You must discover it for yourself.

What I can say about wonder and this pose is that it won't let me stuff myself into a smaller shape, just to stay in my comfort zone or to look like the women who grace my Insta feed. In fact, wheel pose compels me to be *bigger*. I puff out my chest as I lean back. I feel the strength of my arms. I feel strong and powerful, period. And, steady in the pose, I always savor kicking one foot up towards the sky as if I'm walking on the moon's surface. And who knows, maybe one day I will.

But, tonight, as the moon walked me back towards David playing his heart out, I had only three little words: "I don't know." And, for the first time ever, it felt safe to say them. Not just safe, actually—necessary. This confession of uncertainty will, I know, open up an infinite universe for me right here on Earth. The world of touring, my station in life as a wife, daughter, t-shirt seller, executive, and yogi is complicated and colossal, and it's okay to not always know if I'm performing any of it or none of it perfectly; indeed, something in the moon, and everything in yoga, reminds me that I don't need to be performing at all; that all of this will be tested, again and again, but that the only real grade that will be given is the grade I give myself. I don't feel lost in this expanse of space either because, even if I can't hold it in my hands or frame its diploma on my wall, I can bend backwards, and know as Sagan once said that the vastness of what I don't understand will all be "bearable by love."

Kindness

Eka Pada Raja Kapotasana
One-Legged King Pigeon Pose

9

Tupelo Honey

During our Traffic Jam tour season, David had the brilliant idea to invite his oldest friend, Terry, out on the road with us. The two go back to David's recording days at Columbia Records in the early 70s, an era legendary for lascivious shenanigans in the L.A. rock-and-roll scene. From the stories I've heard, David and Terry were not only in the thick of it but also thick as thieves in their escapades, which gives me shivers to think of what's been kept secret. God forgive the havoc they wreaked; Lord have mercy on their party animal spirits. That they're both still alive is miraculous enough. That they're still friends and have been for almost 50 years practically makes Terry kin.

But Mr. Terry Cohen, or *Terriss*, as he prefers the ladies call him, is that member of the family you sit as far away from as possible at Christmas dinner. There are perhaps no two people on the planet more opposite than he and I. I'm sensitive—some (okay, most) might say overly so—while Terry is completely carefree. I don't necessarily mean this in a good way. The only thing we have in common is our bestie.

Spiritual teachers suggest we see "God in all people" but I was certain Terry was the exception. In my estimation, nothing was even remotely redeeming about the man; he was barely *human*. He hails from Chicago and is one-part gangster and a thousand parts playboy. Brazen and unabashed, he takes up the whole room even when he isn't in one. In his youth, he looked like Omar Sharif, a *handsome* Omar Sharif. He was deadly gorgeous, so much so his looks were essentially a weapon. Even now, with his ability to speak with confidence and ease, he makes people not only want to listen to him, but also believe every word he says. (Honestly, it's pretty magical to witness.) He once had an insatiable appetite for food, women, and any sort of stimulant. Back in the day, this posed a particular threat for anyone around him, because he could, and often would, talk you into basically anything. Maybe this quality of salesmanship is why David saw to it to have Terry work the merch table with yours truly.

But I had my suspicions. Maybe David was just trying to amuse himself at my expense; the mere thought of Terry and me manning the same merch table was cause for hilarity. This actually made more sense, because otherwise the choice to have us work together defied logic.

Terry is still reasonably charming at the age of 72, and his God-given good looks have endured, in spite of tipping the scales somewhere around 275. He still has a full head of beautiful hair. His wardrobe is still exceptional, too: dress shirts by Ralph Lauren and Luigi Borrelli, pressed slacks by Armani. Gucci loafers. I mean, he looks regular enough—even striking—but his personality! He's such a beast, I thought; he really shouldn't be out in public.

It was bad enough I had to tolerate him at band meals in commissary, but now I actually had to interact with him, in a job I already absolutely hated. I didn't even have a frame of reference for somebody like Terry Cohen. I'd never met anybody so crass and offensive. There was nothing acceptable about this. The only reason I had the strength to withstand the first week of what I dubbed The Terry Tour was because I was determined to prove to David what a horrible man his best friend was. Well, maybe two; by sheer contrast, I'd show him how perfectly fabulous I could be.

My ingenious plot didn't go so well.

My sweet little merch table, all tidy in its set-up, was organized by categories: hats, CDs, albums, t-shirts. I had fancy printed prices and full-content product descriptions. Our display was even color-coordinated to ensure maximum visual appeal for our buyers. But now, all my hard work and do-gooding was in ruins, held hostage by the smoking cigarettes, telling crude jokes, divulging the details of his latest bowel movement Mr. Cohen.

I was revolted, and growing more neurotic by the second. I tried to ignore him. I tried to disappear into Facebook. I tried to take another coffee break, only to return to crowds, 50 people deep, around

Terry's end of the table, where he leaned back in his chair and regaled them with Viagra-dosing stories or that time he hooked up with you-know-who at one of Clive Davis's parties.

I didn't know if it was shock or bold truth telling but people—men and women, young and old, high society and live-in-the-alley-by-the-stage-door—were and are immediately drawn to Terry. At the merch table, they laughed and hugged and slapped-on-the-back with him and his no-filter ways; they became tour pals, road friends, beer buddies. They bought him drinks and popcorn and chocolate bars, they invited him to watch the show with them, they exchanged phone numbers and promised to have him over the next time he was in town. The whole world loved and loves Terry Cohen. I felt like a freak because I didn't.

This terrific bonding he did with Dave fans happened every single night. I was fascinated at first. Then hot green jealousy seeped in. How was it possible they could love him over Little Miss Sunshine? *Hey, I'm standing right here, ya know. Maybe I'd like a box of licorice or something.* Instead I just smiled and smiled. *T-shirt? Or maybe a signed CD?*

"A cheerful heart is good medicine, but a crushed spirit dries the bones," says Proverbs 17.22. Sages from every walk of faith tell us kindness and good cheer are salves in matters of unease. Jesus wasn't kidding around when he instructed us to love one another. I like to think of myself as sweet as tupelo honey; an angel of the first degree. But it was messy on my insides and messier at our merch table and to put it bluntly, with Terry, my upbeat nature went right out the effing window.

Five days into The Terry Tour, we were in Ft. Lauderdale for a sold-out show in a lovely, upscale performing arts venue. I always took these things very seriously, even more so when they were at places that evoked class with a capital C. But when I got to the merch table—my own little, pretty, on-the-road boutique—I found that the t-shirts had lost their orderly stacks and perfect folds. Again. The CDs were strewn about, again. Our baseball caps hadn't been replenished, *again.* I attempted, for the millionth time, to keep our booth proper and professional, hustling about before an audience member walked by and saw the preschool playground that had been made of my masterpiece. Taking my frustrations out on a heap of Dave tees, I reached underneath the table to find a number of sinister developments: Reese's Pieces wrappers, cigarette butts, stained hot dog cartons, empty coffee cups, crushed soda cans. Terry frequented the concession stand with incredible gusto, in addition to getting showered with food gifts. He ate, like, *all the time*. I sighed, loud enough for him to hear, which was frankly the point. He glanced over at me from his end of the merch table, where he sat wolfing down a Klondike Bar.

Unfriendliness doesn't necessarily have a language. Rather, it's a taut undercurrent. Between bites of his ice cream bar, Terry boomed, "Relax, will ya?," which is one of the worst things to say to someone on the edge, ever.

I dropped the t-shirt I was so carefully folding, burst into tears, and ran sobbing through the lobby and down the side of the theater. I cleared security and landed backstage, out of breath and choking on tears. *David!* I wailed, just as he was about to step on stage. I was looking for empathy, a simpatico, but David just rolled his eyes, grabbed his telecaster, and advised me to get over it quickly or this would be a *very* long tour. He disappeared behind the curtain before I could yell "I quit," which was a waste of breath anyway because the first song was already in full roar. He looked back at me from the stage and winked. Winked! Confirmation, I was sure, that this entire tour with Terry was a conspiracy to watch the nice girl implode.

All honey is sweet but tupelo honey is a different breed. It's derived from trees of the same name—splendid, deciduous trees that thrive in Florida and Georgia. Its flavor is distinct—a little nutty, plenty mild—and it's the only honey that doesn't crystallize. Van Morrison sang of a girl who was as sweet as this honey could be, and he wasn't, I'll tell you, singing about me.

Full disclosure: I have trouble being kind to those I have difficulty with—not because of their behavior—but because of mine. I'm not naturally all that sweet. I've had to work for its authenticity, and I usually dish it out to people I feel are deserving. I come from a culture that wasn't very forgiving; there wasn't a lot of room for errors. Not only was the threat of burning in hell constantly looming over my head, but there was also the possibility of getting thrown off the social registrar for such infractions as eating with the wrong fork or accidentally calling an elder "Bill" instead of "sir." I have clear-cut ideas about how people should act in public, and Terry broke just about all of the rules I'd been adhering to since infancy.

Fake sweet, though—now that I can muster. One has to, if they've ever worked in retail (check) or were raised as a Southern belle (check again) or have to interact with luminaries often (check, check, check). My bouncy, agreeable behavior—my performatively gracious conduct—has become so ingrained that it wasn't until *Terriss* joined us on tour that I realized how blind and pervasive it had become. And yet, it still wasn't cutting it. Around him, I couldn't crystallize anything kind, anyway, even if Jesus himself was standing right over me and demanding it.

Long before The Terry Tour, I coveted not licorice from Dave fans but One-Legged King Pigeon Pose, wherein you touch your back toes to your head while your pelvis is on the floor. It's a dramatic pose; stunning, too, as it showcases one's pliability. I wanted that backbend something bad.

But in order to nail it, I had to learn to quit hating the fact that my lower back wouldn't allow such a drastic manipulation of its innate capacities. It was pesky, my sacrum, jamming into a place where it yelled at me, *this is enough, crazy lady*. I pushed against it anyway, which not only thwarted me from achieving the full expression of the pose but also made me nearly weep in pain in other postures.

It's hard to stay grounded and keep your hips and heart open. It's hard to do your job as a merch girl and be friendly to all you encounter. It all takes an earnest, steadfast commitment; a certain learning of how to soften your edges. I had to learn to befriend this uncooperative and imperfect aspect of my body instead of pretending that I could override it. "Every shortcut is an illusion," Desikachar says, which runs counter to just about everything in our contemporary culture, as well as in Terry's merch-managing standards.

While I've worked up to opening the front of my spine enough to grab my foot with two hands and touch the sole of it to the back of my head, I also can't just crank my body into it. It takes some prep time, some hip opening, some back bending, some love. I couldn't just embrace a friendship with Terry, either. He was so flawed, I thought; so *wild*. He ignited the devilish hate and jealousy that were well and alive inside of me.

Heart opening wasn't easy (then or ever) because things have to change in order for it to happen. I just wasn't that flexible yet. My left shoulder was grouchy and so was my view of how Terry should fold shirts and live in this world. He should quit smoking, I thought. He should keep his mouth shut about anything that happens below the belt. He should eat more greens. He should use his inside voice—wait, does he even have one?

Convinced of this, that it was all too much for me to bear a moment longer, I marched back to the battleground of our merch table, armed with the camera ready on my iPhone, fully intending to gather damning evidence against Terry so David would kick him off the tour and maybe out of our lives. But as I rounded the lobby corner, I saw him refolding the shirts, his face actually *thoughtful*. I stopped cold in my stilettos. My feet ached against the stone lobby floor but my heart felt a warm sliver of an opening.

"You can't stop us on the road to freedom, You can't stop us 'cause our eyes can see," Morrison sings. This is what the yogis say too. All our pain is a matter of *avidya*, which translates to not seeing clearly. It wasn't true that Terry couldn't fold shirts. It wasn't true that Terry didn't care. It wasn't true that Terry was the enemy. The problem was my dogged insistence on perfection.

I've read countless biographies of lives I admire, and I've been shrunk by therapists in examination of my own. I've studied the Bible, the *Bhagavad Gita*, the Big Book of AA. I've devoured an embarrassing number of self-help books. I've amassed a wall full of diplomas, degrees, and professional certifications. I've nested as well as globe-trotted. I've exercised my body to a natural size 2 and faked my breasts to an unnatural size D. I've looked for...*things* on my yoga mat, in clothing boutiques, and in bottles of wine. I'm a seeker in the most literal sense and what irked me—what drove me batty—was that Terry seemed to have conquered what all my striving couldn't deliver: Ease of character. Comfort in his skin. The confidence to take up space. The surety that everyone around him would be keen on hearing what he had to say. While I struggled to fit in with the strangers we came across on the road, I also couldn't sit quietly on my own for two seconds without feeling the crush of fear and shame. Terry, meanwhile, ambled giddily through the world, grinning like he meant it, effortless even with his flaws, completely unfettered.

Terry reminded me that I could be high-strung, uptight, a little snooty, resentful of hard work, and rather entitled in my own way of doing things, even when displaying t-shirts. It was hard to face these imperfections in myself because, hello, I was conscious of them as a yogi and did my best to burn them away through more positive patterns of thinking. But in Terry's presence, they bounced back at me as if I were looking in some fun house mirror. Far easier to call this rumbling, laughing, thundering man unseemly. Appalling. Crazy.

But is there anything crazier than t-shirts that have to be lined up exactly, color-coordinated, with little signs placed precisely one inch to the left? What's sane about insisting that my foot touching the back of my head makes me a superior person? What's sweet about being a snob to everybody on tour?

I saw all of this. I also saw why the first suggestion in the yoga sutras is *maître*, or friendliness; a lesson on how we might sweeten our hardness. The Dalai Lama says, "Be kind whenever possible." To this he adds, "It's always possible." The road to freedom can't be traveled until we've considered the possibility—even probability—that holding our hearts tight keeps us shackled and stingy. To love freely welcomes in diverse ways of being—scrappy manners, definitely not 70%-cacao ice cream bars and all.

Aadil Palkhivala said, "Yoga doesn't care about what you have been; yoga cares about the person you are becoming." Terry was starting to show me that a Dave Mason merchandise table is, in the

Wonder

is the foundation

of yoga.

❖ *Vismayo Yoga Bhumikah*
Shiva Sutras 1.12

end, an altar. It's a dais that conveys kindness and hospitality and inclusion, as over this 4-foot table of goods we meet hundreds of people from all walks of existence. Terry stopped his insane monologues long enough to ask people their names. To inquire about their families. To find out where they worked. To make them feel special. He'd reach his hand, no matter where that hand had been, across the table. He didn't stand off to the side of the human race, silently judging; he joined them. He didn't connect to people through CDs and shirts; he connected with them through his whole, huge, disorderly, sweet heart. He let everybody in.

Including, I realized, me. "Look here, all fixed!" he bellowed across the lobby and with a grand gesture pointed to the table where the t-shirts looked more like a mound of dirty laundry than designer tour shirts. The ushers milling around the foyer started to laugh. The candy vendor shouted, "Good job, Terry!" I felt close to tears again—frantic, really, in how I'd made a mountain out of a molehill—but kept walking towards him anyway.

"Come here, girl," he said, and pulled me in for a bear hug. I closed my eyes against the disaster on the table and the mustard stain on his linen shirt and the glob of what appeared to be relish on his leg (with Terry, you can never be sure). He smelled like Marlboros and an over-application of expensive cologne. For a moment, I didn't care. I felt his heart against mine, the thud thud thud of what it meant to be one.

Terry was out on tour with us for an entire year. I've never laughed so much in my life. While I can't claim it was sweet all the time—like One-Legged King Pigeon Pose, I had to cozy up to him on the daily—but the friendliness between us was as powerful as it was playful. I grew to love Terry and his unbridled joy. Hell, I even missed him.

Because one day, Terry decided he'd had enough of touring. Just as he floated in, he drifted right back out. He's in Chicago again, making other people laugh.

Several tour seasons have passed since then, and rarely does a show go by without someone stopping by the merch table, not to buy something but to ask, "Hey, where's Terry?" as if he were some lost king. I field questions about him not because I have to but because I'm warming up to the idea that God does indeed exist in all people—and that once we nail this knowledge, everything turns out sweet.

Gratitude

Anjali Mudra
Salutation Seal

10

Sunshine Of Your Love

There's something powerful about holding your attention on your own hands. Not halfway attention, like one eye on the merch booth and one eye on the guest I'm chatting with while also texting my little brother in California and admiring a cool pair of boots walking by. I mean real, sustained, meaningful attention.

I used to have this gift, at least when it came to work and the sleekest, glossiest blowout I could manage without stepping into a salon. But since I've been on tour, I've gotten good at dividing my energy. *Too* good, because it's coming at a cost. I'm scattered, unfocused, and ungrounded; a little more depleted every day. One minute I'm scheduling an interview for David in Toledo and the next I'm *in* Toledo and can't figure out what, precisely, happened in the tornado in between. If I wanted to feel this way I might as well have kept my job as an art dealer, a career that had me running four galleries in three states. More pay, less travel, earlier nights. A house that didn't come with a steering wheel.

I once prized myself not only for my fierce focus but also, ironically, for my ability to multitask. I could handle a fragile artist on one hand and make a huge sale for them on the other; I could check my email while doing my mascara while *driving*. (Don't try it.) I did all of this while also chatting with the customers who walked through the gallery's doors and ensuring that each boutique was in tiptop shape, my house gleamed floor to ceiling, and my manicure was perfection. It wasn't until I walked—no, trudged—into that first yoga class that I realized how thoroughly draining my whole hustle was.

Modern neuroscience tells us that no matter what job you're doing, the mind can't process more than one task at a time. This makes me feel better about being so slow to add up the price of a CD, a hat, and a photo. I thought it was my poor math skills, something that's haunted me since childhood and is undoubtedly amplified after four consecutive shows and the sleepless nights that often accompany them. It's hard, this. I know it's along the lines of crying from the yacht—most of the time, I realize how fortunate I am—but I'm trying to do math and be gracious to our wonderful guests and standing in the cold at 11:49pm while also trying to remember what city we're in and what day of the week it is and where David's stage glasses might be and what kind of mood he'll be in. I'm trying to do all of this when half of my heart isn't even here on tour. It's over there...in the yoga world.

I'm like only *half in love* out here. Ravi Ravindra said, "It is the lack of a love affair that makes everything stale, dull, and uninteresting," and I don't think he was talking exclusively about lovers. It's no wonder, then, that my divided attention, my less-than-wholehearted-engagement on this particular tour, is making life feel simultaneously over-stimulated and humdrum. "A house divided against itself cannot stand," Abraham Lincoln once said. Internal dissention will bring down a government as sure as it will crush your spirit.

Yogis suggest the cultivation of attention—or mindfulness—as medicine for emotional healing and the stresses of everyday life. It lights us up from the inside and makes exactly where we are rich and edifying; less angst-y. Older than religion, the practice, as we all know, is having its moment today. Mindfulness is the spiritual new black, a salve to all problems and every occasion. Millennials, bless their sweet, hopeful souls, use it instead of *drinking*. Versions of it are everywhere, too: apps on my phone, books on my nightstand, covers on magazines I scan in line as I pick up beer for the band, whole hours on podcasts I listen to, and even on t-shirts, which admittedly I wear myself. ("Heavily Meditated" is my current fave.) And while the benefits of mindfulness are undeniable, it can also begin to feel like just another thing to achieve. In this world of soul-enhancement and self-improvement and poreless skin, the practice can turn in on itself and promote striving instead. On top of everything I have to do, now I have to be mindful? Act like a yogi off the mat, even if I'm caffeine deprived and jetlagged and irked by the way David talks to me when he's overwhelmed? Always be kind and patient, even to someone in line at the merch table who has most definitely had too much to drink? Compassionate and friendly, to *everyone*? Focused? It's no surprise I'm exhausted.

To be real, the pursuit of mindfulness just makes me feel bad about myself because I'm decidedly not any of those things all of the time, especially on days when I hit the downward toboggan run towards shame and defeatism—the usual suspects, in my case, as a result of too little sleep and a road-weary body. (Who am I kidding—sometimes just because it's a Tuesday.) It's difficult to track the source of this darkness, which, therapists say, is ultimately what will put mental demons to rest. But what I know for sure is that I can't multitask crankiness and loveliness.

I'm barely hanging on in this present ride through the East Coast. Our string of concerts starts in Florida, runs through the Carolinas, and shoots through Maryland, Pennsylvania, New Jersey, New York, Massachusetts, and Maine. You'd think that, as a yogi, I'd know how to not burn myself out; how to avoid the crispy action of frying my brain from overwork and the flight from my body that comes with it. Even if I wasn't a yogi, I should know from experience. I've been a worker bee since college, laying my hands on my first real job three days after I tossed my graduation cap and hardly stopping since. (Those days in rehab were a different kind of work entirely.) Sure, I'd had summer jobs before my resume officially began—my father was a big proponent of a Strong Work Ethic—but my first "grown-up" job set up a pattern of desperately trying to prove myself worthy of a paycheck.

Alas, here I am again, only this time it's trickier and messier, with a whole lot more emotion involved—a byproduct of working with and for your spouse, who also happens to be the star of the show and therefore the CEO, and I'm not after a paycheck so much as I am his adoration and respect. This is made even thornier when my real, non-person love, I'm convinced, rests not inside a freezing-ass concert hall in Boston but in a spacious studio lined with sunlit windows, a bright yoga teacher at the front guiding me through the poses I so love. Messier still is that on top of my day AND night job of touring, I'm trying to figure out this thing called life from an open-hearted, gentle, humble, and *mindful* place. I am, in the end, a workaholic obsessed with securing spiritual nirvana and an A+ in pure thoughts, perfect actions, and wife-dom.

Talk about internal dissention. Talk, too, about a foolproof way to fall out of the present and live in resentment.

Awareness in the here and now attached to striving—this mindfulness that I must, must, must accomplish—is different than awareness attached to appreciation and curiosity. It's the difference between resisting that second jelly donut backstage in Philadelphia because you know it's not "a healthy choice" and investigating why the jelly donut has a magnetic superpower over you even though you're not hungry and frankly don't even like jam in your donuts, anyway. Once I remove obligatory mindfulness from the equation, experiencing the here and now is actually quite fascinating—whether I'm looking at donuts or the hands that hold them.

Human hands are unique. No other earthly creature can grasp, hold, or manipulate like us. According to Aristotle, the hand is the "tool of tools." There is the laying of hands, the raising of one's hand, lending a hand, hand on the heart, hands on your hips, hands down, hand-it-to-ya, I wanna hold your hand. Our hands communicate volumes without speaking a word. The mere position of them has the ability to influence energy. They can summon or dismiss, invite or threaten, grasp or release, let go or love.

They're also amazingly complex and sensitive. There are 2,500 nerve receptors per square centimeter in each one of our hands. Each of our fingers has nerve terminals connected to our endocrine glands—you know, those things that regulate our hormones and metabolism. Biology aside, yogis say our hands are the motor organ of our heart; the outward expression of our deepest feelings. They flow with information we can actually feel, both on the giving and receiving ends. 108 meridians run directly out of our *anahata* chakra and into our hands, so that when we touch others—or anything, really, even that sticky, sugary donut—we do so with our hearts. It's how we convert intention into action; it's how we do our *real* soul's work on this planet.

Hence why yoga practices focus on the alignment of your heart, because this is how we work—this is how we connect—in the world. All yoga happens in relationship, and there is no separation between how we're treating ourselves and how we act with others. How we are loving, after all, is how we are living.

I'm a Gemini, always in search of her twin, that "something missing" that will render me whole. This leads to an absurd amount of envy, an outrageous capacity to exist in two places at the same time, a tendency to accidentally overlook the beauty of what's in front of me, and a near-criminal knack for absconding the present while I'm standing right in front of you. "He is a wise man who does not grieve for the things which he has not, but rejoices for those which he has," the Greek philosopher Epictetus wrote. He's right, of course. Gratitude may be as trendy as mindfulness, but it's just as important. The problem is, gratitude eludes me out here on tour. What is there to be grateful for? This is hard work, the donuts suck, we're always on the go, and David holds his guitar a lot more than he holds my hand. No wonder my mind is elsewhere.

Yoga gives me the chance to work on this in a tangible way. The practice draws our attention inward, a counter-pose to the usual demands of outward-facing daily life. Even the most rigorous vinyasa classes ask us to settle into a pose for a while; to stay where we are and see what happens when we connect the whole body with the whole mind and make the necessary adjustments for a full, strong expression. All of this is the converse of the go-go-go sensibility I soaked up in the fine art world for decades, but maybe that's why yoga called to me in the first place. It feels good to stop feeling split between this task and that one; this musician and him over there; the desire to be as healthy as possible and to eat my body weight in donuts. Yoga is a constant coming home to the stillest, quietest room in the house.

But making gestures with our hands, a practice yogis call mudras, can be surprisingly difficult. I can find a world of hurt just trying to make my fingers bend in new and unusual ways, just like I can in trying to bend my life into living on a bus selling loot to a thousand people and alongside an artist who is so squarely in *his* jam and feeling farther and farther away from my own—as a resident of a home that doesn't come with a gas pedal and a member of a stationary community and, perhaps above all, as a yoga teacher, demonstrating these tough mudras to others.

Anjali Mudra is the one gesture that comes easily to me, in class and in life. You simply place your palms and wrists together and hold your hands at your heart. It's one of the most common mudras, and it crosses language and cultural barriers. It unites people around the world; it's the universal gesture of gratitude.

"Gratitude unlocks the fullness in life," Melody Beattie says. She also says that it "turns what we have into enough, denial into acceptance, chaos into order, confusion into clarity." *Anjali* translates "to offer" or "to salute." The practice of this mudra, then, encourages the practitioner to get centered and still by aligning the heart with gratitude. Healer and sage Krishnamacharya attested to this, saying, "This gesture signified the potential for an intention to progress to greatest spiritual awakening. When done properly the palms are not flat against each other; the knuckles at the base of the fingers are bent a little. Creating space between the palms and fingers of the two hands, resembling a flower yet to open, symbolizes the blooming of our hearts."

This is all wise and inspiring, but in the frenetic pace and constricted reality of tour life, creating a little open space in any capacity is nothing short of a miracle, and when it happens in my heart I call it relief. And yet, when I'm sitting on my mat between chaturangas and warriors, or sitting aboard our bus between Atlanta and Aspen, or sitting on a flight between Maui and Reno, what helps bear the weight of this kind of stretch, the place between where I am and the place where I am going?

I'm starting to see that stretches of any kind are a route back towards ourselves. Like the two sides of the hands that meet in Anjali Mudra, the two sides of my soul's path, the touring and my yoga

A cheerful heart is good medicine, but a crushed spirit dries the bones.

✦ *Proverbs 17.22*

practice, myself and my wandering, restless twin—even me and David—are more powerful when they're joined together in the present moment; when they're attentive and 100% in my heart. The heart is a muscle, remember. Western scientists describe it as an "involuntary muscle" but I take issue with that portrayal. When we pay attention, there's nothing "involuntary" at all. We have a huge choice when it comes to matters of the heart. We can be open and welcoming and appreciative, or we can be closed off and ungenerous and bitter. We can stay in the shade we ourselves have usually made or cross over into the sunshine.

Rock lore has it that the beat poet Pete Brown wrote the first line of Cream's "Sunshine Of Your Love" when, after being up all night working, Jack Bruce played a riff inspired by Jimi Hendrix. Later, Eric Clapton—then a guitarist for Cream—wrote the iconic bridge of the song, *I've been waiting so long, To be where I'm going, In the sunshine of your love.* The song as a whole is hard rock, psychedelia, and pop, all at once. Music theorists call it the precursor of Led Zeppelin and heavy metal. It was one of the biggest hits of the 60s, no matter that Ahmet Ertugen once said that it was too experiential to flourish.

What does this tell me? That collaboration is key to anything meaningful, of course, whether that's a collaboration between your mind and your heart or between a husband and a wife. But it also tells me that every world, no matter how different, informs the other, and letting this dialogue play out is all part of the fun we should be grateful for having. Would I really be as expressive on the mat if my commitment to yoga wasn't offset by the rock-and-roll world? Would I cherish David's loving attention, when it happens, if we didn't bicker about making a stop (*please please please*) at Louis Vuitton? Would I want to stay sober and awake at every concert if I hadn't gone through the opposite? Would my solid-black outfit look bland if it didn't have a splash of color? (Naturally.)

Indeed, in some ways living a tour life, which by definition is a life that journeys from place to place, is karmically perfect for a person who struggles with gratitude and with feeling at home in her own skin. Six-hour bus drive? Thank you! Another tray of deli sandwiches? Thank you! Leaving David's favorite shirt at the venue? Thank you! David getting mad at me for leaving said shirt? Thank you! The practice of gratitude, the universe is trying to tell me, can't be selective.

"I'm with you love," the song says, and when I can do that—when that "you" is this moment that I ought to be so appreciative of—I feel like I'm nourished by some indefinable warmth; I feel that I, too, am on my way towards blooming. Gratitude anchors me amidst spiritual discomfort. It drenches the moment with a certain brightness and focus. It shines light within and reveals wholeness, serving as a loving reminder that the twin I'm looking for, or any parts of myself I'm missing, couldn't possibly be Out There. Being thankful for who and where I am allows me to become available and receptive, so that when love and abundance want to touch down, they can land on me rather than having me chase them down, or, worse, whooshing right over me like a windstorm. Like right now, when I'm concentrating on getting to Charleston with David's interviews checked off and over in the done column so I can put together his VIP folders in time to meet these people at precisely 5:15 with a genuine smile and a firm handshake. Sometimes I will be a little out of breath or a little out of balance; so what? I never have been afraid of hard work. I get to make a living and hang out with my husband, see friends, see the country, see concerts, AND see my hands, whatever they might be doing.

"Keep your face always toward the sunshine and shadows will fall behind you," Walt Whitman wrote. Gratitude, like sunshine, is said to elevate your mood and lower your blood pressure. Sun salutations, which we yogis practice, classically start and end with Anjali Mudra. They're a method of awakening energy; to bring you to the present. Anjali Mudra, meanwhile, helps you realize that your sunshine is precisely where your hands land: Inside your heart.

Cream played "Sunshine Of Your Love" as their encore—their way of giving thanks to the audience—at their historic reunion concert at the Royal Albert Hall in London in 2005. I wasn't in the audience but I'm sure that in this case, I would have been pinned to the moment; I would have gone wild. Why? Because remarkable moments do that. But I'm also beginning to see that mundane moments can be just as exquisite. It comes down to unclenching your fists and taking in the details, however grim or glorious. It's in breathing in this raucous music of life in and around you. It's sitting long enough in a single spot to let the sun wash over you, as if to say, this journey, love, is *exactly* the right direction.

Service

Padmasana

Lotus

11

Listen To The Music

Yoga strives to widen our perception by calling attention to our heart, where we can make the unseen seen, because, as Antoine de Saint-Exupery said, "It is only with the heart that one sees rightly. What is essential is invisible to the eye." Hanging out for even just a few breaths in a yoga pose shows me tight spots I was completely unaware of; places where my heart needs to expand.

Like a yoga posture held for more than a few seconds, inhabiting a tour life for more than just a couple of shows brings up layers of hidden pain, lurking there below the superficial. More than just the physical body, according to the Taittiriya Upanishad, there are four more layers, each subtler than the rest, and each interlaced and interactive so that movement in one of these affects all the others. To sit in silence and stillness, away from distraction, looks simple enough. In truth, though, the very act often causes those concealed hurts to rise to the surface. They emerge in lotus pose on the Prevost and they appear in my seat at the merch table before the show ends and they start shrieking at me while I'm drinking coffee alone backstage. No organic half and half? Only powdered creamer? (Really, what's the point of coffee at all under these circumstances?) As a chronic do-er, all this waiting—all this unexpected quiet on a rock-and-roll tour, of all places—rouses the monsters inside me and creates a sudden, nearly visceral ache.

Sages from all spiritual disciplines declare that it is our heartache that helps us grow into new possibilities and fresh opportunities. I must be honest: this feels like mere platitude. It reminds me of my wedding day (to my first husband), when, during a sudden downpour, my maid of honor cheerily quipped, "Well, you know, rain on your wedding day is a sign of great luck!" *Right, of course.*

Heartache itself, I believe, isn't the path—it's a pit stop. Pain is not a method of practice. I say this because no sooner had I set out on my first tour that I became *painfully aware* I'd made a mistake. Midweek, mid-day, in the middle of that first run, halfway through a Styrofoam cup of powdered creamed coffee in one hand and my cell phone in the other, I reached out to one of my yogi friends back in California looking for relief, some wise and helpful counsel to ease my aching heart. But "everything happens for a reason" didn't cut it. I suspected the worst. She confirmed my fears with the universal buzzwords for *you're basically screwed.*

I had little room, really, to navigate that tight spot, that feeling that I'd made a terrible decision; that I'd been kicked off the path I was supposed to be on and shoved onto another rougher route—one that clearly wasn't meant for the likes of me.

What met my eyes most days were my own tears. I could call it loneliness, but in truth it was a case of self-pity and of a heart hardened by snap judgments of other people. It takes effort, some actual searching, some actual *feeling*, to go below the surface of a situation or a person. Not me; I'd rather cling to pain and appearances. I marched forward, one foot in front of the other, city after city after city, wearing my all-access tour laminate like a badge of *pain-is-my-practice* honor, feeling like I had no access to this world at all.

The paradox of working on a tour is that there is very little actual attending of the shows. I'm in too thick and in too close, getting bogged down in counting shirts and fetching throat lozenges. It's all too easy to forget about the music. Perspective gets blunted in service to petty details; meaning and purpose get lost. I disappear into the details; I can't even remember what I came out on tour to do.

The paradox of presence, meanwhile, is that the real is revealed when the mind gets out of its own way. One of Patanjail's yoga sutras defines the practice as the quieting of the mind for the purpose of experiencing the calm, observant self that exists deep within. We don't engage in such a high state of consciousness by default. We're too engrossed in mundane affairs to have the capacity to hear our genuine, objective selves. Our internal chatter is too loud to hear God.

And yet, we must believe that such music is there in order for us to do, well, anything. While our minds are complex and multi-layered—even, dare I say, magnificent—they're also too small to see the rich, magical, invisible weave of life. Unless we pause to access different stations, to listen to and service something bigger than ourselves, we may think that what we see is what we get. This is about as true as thinking a downpour on your wedding day is good luck. Just because I've seen Savannah, Georgia, on a map and read all about what to see and where to eat there, it's not the same as experiencing the uneven feel of her cobblestone streets, or the romantic charm of the weeping Spanish moss. We must forget what we think we know and dissolve into the present.

Asmita, often translated as ego, is the me-ness of grandeur on one side, or vulnerable inadequacy on the other. It frames our world as we think it should look like; it tells us how it should all go down. No matter how you slice it, it's a distorted sense of viewing the world. Ravi Ravindra teaches it as "attachment to the small." At the same time, Marianne Williamson reminds us that "playing small doesn't serve the world."

Music is similar to yoga in that it all happens in relationship. The delicate manner in which notes are played together is as magical and necessary as the bond between the musicians and the audience. Yoga often translates as *union* or *connection*, and sages say everything in the universe is linked. *We are all one*. "Nonsense!" yells the ego, which resides in the superficial and always sees the self as separate from others. But what's to love about a one-chord song?

Oneness is hard enough to believe in from a physical point of view; after all, you and I are clearly different people. We have our own ideas about what makes a good cup of coffee and likely have different opinions on the best Beatles song.

But what we likely will agree upon is the power of music, the splendor and enchantment of a good song. It can switch the channel, so to speak, of our own mental chatter, which for most people, whether you know it or not, is always on. Don't think that's true? Then try to sit down and do a little meditating and see what happens.

Because the mind is always playing some kind of tune, yogis use the practice of mantra, which is a syllable, a sound, a word, or a group of words—a mini-song, if you will—as a means to free the mind. Mantra translates as "mind protection," which begs the question, what are we protecting our minds *from*? Those unconscious, invisible thoughts that natter away inside of us, of course. And mine, when I first went on tour, were acting like those buff, armed security guards who escort David through the crowds after the show. They make sure you and I don't connect.

Tom Johnston of The Doobie Brothers wrote in "Listen To The Music" that "what the people need is a way to make them smile, it ain't so hard to do if you know how." It's a song that reminds us we're all in this together; some of us happy, some of us sad, it doesn't matter. What matters is how we are connecting to each other. This is the service we offer to each other, even if we don't realize it. The well-being of humanity is our own well-being. It's what Ram Dass meant when he said that we are all here "walking each other home."

On tour, we sing and dance our audience home. There's an undeniable, uplifting energy to a concert. And one evening, I decided to surrender to it, which is what you eventually have to do when you've outgrown the small little world you've been living in. I got a bucket of popcorn and a seat in the back of the theater, where I listened to the music like any other ticketholder and not like the musician's, I-think-I-belong-better-in-the-yoga-world's wife. I let those songs become mantras, and as my defenses came crashing down, my connection with those around me increased. First it was the people I was seated next to. Then it was our whole section. By the end of the show, I was on my feet and dancing and singing with all 1,500 of them.

Now, maybe it was the dim room, but maybe it was mantra; whatever "it" was, these newfound dance partners suddenly didn't look so different than me. Maybe we wore different clothes, maybe there was an age difference, a gender difference, hair color or *no hair* difference, but we all left that concert hall a little happier, a little more bonded as card-carrying members of the human race.

I couldn't wait to get to the merch table after that show. Not so much to sell my new compatriots a t-shirt, but to drink a cup of coffee with them and talk about *those songs* we just heard.

"This," I thought to myself, "is the greatest job in the world." Who wouldn't want to be a part of *this*? People leave a yoga class, generally speaking, peaceful and calm—plenty happy, to be sure. But folks leave our shows so ecstatic that they're singing and dancing and hugging and kissing; they are their own music. For a moment—perhaps even two hours—they've been taken away from the superficial and transported to something that's, well, super.

The Dalai Lama said, "When we feel love and kindness toward others, it not only makes others feel loved and cared for. But it helps us also to develop inner happiness and peace." When I'm standing in the lobby immersed in hating where I am and selling CDs, people look more like twenty dollar bills than love. But when I'm no longer defending my sad, small view of the world, I can be more open-hearted to who is in it with me.

One-on-oneness naturally leads to a deeper understanding of Oneness. I discovered that Music is my real boss. I serve the imperceptible, magical *feel good* every bit as much of those flesh and bloods who are making the music—David, the band, and the audience. The agents who book us, the venues who host us, the caterers who feed us. It doesn't stop there. The babysitters who watch the children as parents go out for date night, the farmers who grew the food we eat, the music teacher who taught David to sing. Six degrees of Kevin Bacon no longer seems like a silly parlor game. Invisible connection and service to it is real medicine. Gandhi said, "The best way to find yourself is to lose yourself in the service of others." This seems anything but platitude to me.

Yogis recommend meditation as a way to see yourself so that you can interact with others more compassionately. Classically, the practice is depicted as a seated lotus posture. Because the lotus rises from muddy water to blossom as a flower, it's a symbol of purity and rebirth. Similarly, the practices of meditation are a method of cleaning our thoughts through the alchemical process of rising from the lower to the higher by paying close attention. "In this body are all the Gods and all the Demons," Buddha said. Hips, knees, and low back are all teachers to reckon with when I endeavor to sit in peace and quiet.

It is a slow, sometimes maddening process, but we all know that we often have to go through the dark to get to the light. It's growing and opening enough where the sun can get in. At night, the lotus flower closes its petals, sinks underwater, and each morning it ascends and opens again. The wisdom path, like a tour and like a lotus, travels every day, and ultimately, everything dark is an opportunity to rise. "No mud, no lotus," the yogis say.

Ramana Maharishi said, "Our own self-realization is the greatest service we can render to the world." Which seemed self-centered to me at first. But the experience of being a slave to unconscious thoughts instead of a servant to presence is an altogether different tuning. Whether I'm on a yoga mat or in a backstage hallway, in Bali or in Baltimore, I can find a struggle. The struggle isn't with that powdered coffee creamer, of course. It's with myself. It's sneaky, these thoughts, this music of the mind that plays like white noise. Giving service to low-grade psychic pain isn't helpful to anyone. My self-involved mud is only good as a building block for my own personal transformation of character.

Add sunlight to mud and it turns to dust. An unexpected errand to Ace Hardware for a Phillips head screwdriver can be either be a boring and tedious task, or it can be gratifying when you see it as service because somebody, for some reason, needs it on stage, and needs it right now. *Run as fast as you can and pick up a screwdriver. NOW. Not when you finish your coffee* helps me realize I'm not the center of this operation, but part of a larger show.

Most of the time we'll never know what part we played in the big picture of things, but that seems less and less the point. To offer ourselves to others is a byproduct of feeling safe and secure, unthreatened, and connected, just as it is an indication of faith. "And if I'm feeling good to you and you're feeling good to me. There ain't nothing we can't do or say," sing The Doobies. Feeling good inside, obviously, is awesome. But the greater benefit is that it transforms the world around us to a more easeful and kinder place for everybody.

I now watch as many shows as I can while out on tour. I've heard all those songs hundreds of times; I know them by heart, and I love them more with each and every concert because they spread the invisible, essential ingredient of love to everybody in the room.

And that tool that interrupted my coffee break? It's a part of every show: It secures a bolt in the three-legged stool David uses on stage for certain guitar solos. It's invisible, but I know it's there.

Ease

Parivrtta Janu Sirsasana
Revolved Head-to-Knee Pose

12

Take It Easy

I'm out of touring practice this year, my fourth year as a full-timer. I've taken time off to do house things, and if the truth be told I've been practicing a lot of *loving staying at home*. Our little Maltese Star had 15 of her 42 teeth pulled, and in an effort to get her back into road dog condition—which requires more than a couple of aspirin and a few days off—I've ditched part of our latest tour to stay with her for a few extra weeks.

In my attempt to encourage healing vibes, I've fluffed up our Nevada house by fixing little things here, adding fresh kitchen towels there, decluttering and dialing in details everywhere. If it's true what they say, that "God is in the details," I suppose you could say this refinement in my living space is a way of becoming more at home with God. This requires cultivating ease in my relationship with all of life. *Embrace that which unfolds*, they say, including an almost toothless dog, disgusting dishtowels, and a husband who is all in a huff halfway across the country.

In this cosmic intersection of homesteading and touring—in this pulling together of antithetical ways of living—I'm continually reminded that the most important detail isn't in the right size of a throw rug or the perfect set of steak knives. It's in the ease of being comfortable in your own skin, and the calm with which you can move through the world. You could say I'm searching for the comforts of home inside myself, too. (And in the meantime, I sure do love these external creature comforts.)

But no matter how serene my house may be, I'm still feeling jumpy and mildly tormented, as if there's something that needs to be tended to I can't quite see. This feeling, of course, is the real home to which I've grown accustomed. *Dukkha* is the Sanskrit word for suffering, and somewhere along my path I've come to believe a little suffering is a more "spiritual" and profound way of living. The opposite of *dukkha* is *sukkha*, or ease. Yogic texts are filled with practical information about how to access this state. One might even say it's the main point, as evidenced in Patanjali's second sutra. I want so much to be able to do this. How ridiculous do I sound that I can't? I mean, can anything be easier than ease?

As I travel around the country in various climates and conditions I find that my response to "are you comfortable?" depends on where I am. Not only in terms of a map or a calendar, or what weather the day brings. What have I been eating? How much sleep am I getting? Are David and I engaged in wedded bliss or are we *thisclose* to tearing off each other's heads? The reply to the question of ease depends on what layer of myself is answering.

The Taittiriya Upanishad focuses on the levels of consciousness that make up a person. These *koshas*, of which there are five, often translate as "sheaths," but I've also seen the word translated as "home" and even "plentitude" and "abundance." Two of the four Purusharthas (or "four aims of life") are "prosperity" and "pleasure," right alongside "duty" and "liberation." Sages, it seems, suggest the Self is an abode of peace and plenty.

To which I sometimes want to say, *you're foolin' me.*

Our little dog bounced back after surgery quickly. My outermost kosha, my body, the *annamaya*, wanted to lie to David about this; to tell him our sweet little dog needed at least another month's rest, which, by that time, would be so close to the end of the tour run that I might as well just stay home and see him when he got back. (Right?) I wanted to sink into my comfy couch with a cup of hot tea, a good book, and my happily-recovered dog. Throw another log on the fireplace, admire my new orchids, flip through Better Homes & Gardens, abandon responsibility. I could very well say kaput to the entire tour; surely, David could survive without me.

But those koshas, darn it, those deeper, wiser layers, refused to come along for the ride. They couldn't be put to rest. My heart and soul wouldn't let such deception to David happen. I rolled my eyes at them but my breath became as shallow as my intentions. Our bodies, I saw, really are the temple of the spirit; the only language we can trust.

One definition of yoga is "integration" and there is great power in aligning all the layers of your being. There is also a tremendous sense of ease when you're not pulled in numerous directions. If you think it feels good to find that self-adjustment when your low back finally pops into place, think of the feeling when your lower, greedy, more selfish thoughts give way to love, service, and peace.

All of this results in finding what's known as *dharma*. While it's impossible to precisely translate the ancient Hindu term, some take it to mean as *right alignment*, or the right way of living. In Hawaii, we call this *pono*; in Nevada—and beyond—it's a state of existence characterized by integrity and that feeling of contentment that arrives when we know that what we're doing is charitable, good, and true. The idea behind it is that moral behavior leads to happiness for the doer and everyone around them. To me, it sounds a lot like people-pleasing and codependency. Clearly, I'm failing at *dharma*, and I'm pretty good at ditching my husband to eat bon bons on the couch too.

For wise folks like teacher Ravi Ravindra, *dharma* doesn't come from a place of lack or neediness, both of which I often fall victim to. It doesn't demand someone love you for doing your job. He defines it as a "responsibility for the maintenance of order." It's one's path in life; one's purpose. One's way of being, in accordance with the unspoken laws of the universe. It means striking the right balance in your relationships.

Five koshas. Four aims of life. How are you supposed to give them all equal footing? I can barely stay poised when tempted with new kitchen linens.

I'd like to think that I'm pretty clear on my life's purpose, but it's called into question, again and again, when I'm on tour. Tour life doesn't make "sense." It doesn't gel with my perceived *dharma*, and I'm left second guessing everything. Yoga can be described as "union with the Divine" and I suppose what we have to notice first is that we're disconnected. Taking time off from the tour and hanging out alone with Star in blissful solitude eventually became more contemplative and upsetting than I expected. More serious than making sure I had the right scent of Nest candles and a sturdy enough broom to remove the pine needles from the corners of my wooden deck. Big questions inescapably surfaced. Who am I? What am I doing, really? How do I want to live my life? Why am I on the road with David? Why does the yoga practice mean so much to me? What happens when these seemingly opposite paths clash? I'm not a musician or a groupie; a partier or a social butterfly. I'm an introvert who likes things tidy and quiet. I feel like Arjuna in the first chapter of the *Bhagavad Gita*: a reluctant participant in life's duty.

And yet, how is it possible that, on the other hand, touring feels correct? True? *Right?* Not because it's easy, and not because it's the suffering I find weirdly alluring (at least, I don't suffer all of the time on the road). Rather, touring feels strangely healing.

It takes courage to see yourself clearly and skill and determination to make your life meaningful. The Eagles make it sound so simple. "Just find a place to make your stand, and take it easy," they sing in their classic song. Intellectually, I get this. It's what the yoga sutras say about all postures, after all; that they are a combination of opposites, of effort and ease, of grounding and ascending. *Sthira sukham asanam.*

This wisdom is often offered as a suggestion to bring ease to your efforts, but it's the opposite that commands my attention lately. That is, *can I make the effort to find ease?* And, I don't know, again, isn't that a contradiction?

While I'm on tour, finding ease is an obvious, necessary, and constant practice. I find it by stealing away in the early mornings for a cup of coffee while David and Star are still resting (our other dog Lucy, sadly, passed away during one of our tours). I find it in yoga classes and at unexpected road stops. But my recent "time off" has revealed I'm just as anxiety-ridden at home too. I'm not easeful anywhere, really—not on my mat, not at home, not on tour, not even in a bathtub. I'm anxious almost all of the time, which is kind of a bummer because I've been practicing yoga for nearly two decades. You'd think I'd be more tranquil by now. Cool, calm, collected. More *yoga-like*, for God's sake.

Ease, though, I'm beginning to see, *is* a practice. It's a way of life; it's living our *dharma*. The second the whole of us is in line—when all of those levels of our consciousness are in concert—ease sets in. This is the zone people speak of; that wonderful mental place where everything feels smooth and sincere. Natural.

So why does it elude me? St. Augustine says, "Our heart is restless until it rests in you (God)," and perhaps this is the key. The root of my anxiety isn't the cold and barren Northern Nevada landscape, or the lack of fresh vegetables backstage in Pennsylvania, or even a husband whose worldview is blind to the benefits of cobra pose, although it all sure seems like it when anxiety is upon me. When I strip away surface details, there's a lot of unease because I haven't truly bought into the God thing. I can't rest in God because I can't see him.

"Eyes of the flesh see things of the flesh, eyes of the spirit see things of the spirit," says St. Paul. The practices of yoga are here to help us develop our spiritual eyes. I know this, but I'm starting to wonder if I might need glasses.

The third rung along the eight limb path is *asana*, or physical postures. It's where yoga met me fifteen years ago and it's where it still finds me every day on the mat. *Asana* is powerful because what you're doing in a pose is what you're doing everywhere. It literally stretches you out of your comfort zone, away from what you know and can see, and into newly discovered territory—things that have actually been with you all along but you just haven't seen yet. *Asana* gives us the safest of places—our own body—to practice dealing with the fear of the unknown and her many manifestations. It's the world's greatest gift to anybody with *annamaya kosha* issues. Panic attacks aren't a method of easy living.

Seated poses, in particular, are an antidote for my endless anxiety because I can see and feel the earth beneath me. I feel supported and held, conditions where feeling freaked isn't necessary.

Parivrtta Janu Shirsasana is especially healing. It has the energy of a good long tour because, like life, it's complicated and awkward and a little painful until you unwind the tension. Until you relax into the endeavor.

The pose is an inner thigh extension, a side bend, and a twist all in one. To bring the back of my head to my knee, particularly when my heart revolves away from its natural inclination to bend forward, is triggering. There's a lot to be anxious about when you can't see where to rest your head. This is as true to the pose as it is on tour, when so often our schedule doesn't allow for a lot of rest. When we do finally put our heads to bed, it's often in the middle of the night, in a location we've never seen, in a bed not nearly as nice as the one we have at home.

I can't blame touring for my unease, or anything else for that matter except, as the Eagles sing, "The sound of your own wheels (that) drive you crazy." My own never stop turning. I wish I could quiet them, and so I practice *asana*, again and again, day after day. It works, at times, to reduce the tension in my body and to calm my breath. In turn, the mental trappings of my mind, the deeper layers of the Self, begin to settle down in earnest.

But away from the mat, as I said, I'm often a nervous wreck, and for no foreseeable reason. I sit here on the sofa sipping a cup of green tea, to which I've added clover honey, and the whole moment sweetens as the sun sets out my living room window. From the outside looking in, it's a picturesque scene: Novel, tea, pup, pillows. But it's still enough inside and out to realize I'm in a spin. *RELAX, damn it*, I tell myself, and the silence feels too much in this room.

The ding of my iPhone pulls me off the verge and back into the moment. It's a text from one of David's fans, a man who has been to nearly a hundred of his shows. We're on a first name basis by now. We share not only a love of David but also of peppermint ice cream. "Where are you? The show was amazing, a life changing event!" I admit to myself that I miss it. I miss this friend-fan and the thousand others I would have seen if I'd been out on the road. I miss the laughter. The music. The guys in the band. David. I glance at my watch and figure it's right about the time on the East Coast that he's just gotten off stage, still dripping with sweat from the show. I'm hoping there's somebody close by with a cold towel and a warm heart, who's wrapping his throat, handing him a dry shirt to change into, offering congratulations on another great concert. If I ever wonder what *dharma* looks like in action, I don't have to look much farther than David.

And while it sure feels nice here on the sofa, I know I'm not in *dharma* here either. As lovely as it is to nest, it isn't my life path. Something isn't quite in alignment, my panic tells me this, and I can tell, not because I'm practicing a pose, but because I'm practicing the real yoga. Ease up, I tell myself. Surrender. *Sukkha*. Let Go and Let God.

And my word, the spinning stops. Peace sets in.

Is that you, God? It's me, Winifred.

"Calm is higher than ecstasy," says Ramana Maharshi. The silence all around me says: No need to frantically search for joy or happiness, or even love. No need to be worried you're doing life incorrectly. No need to lie to anybody, especially ourselves, about doing the work in the world to which we're called, even if it doesn't look like what we imagined, or what our mom wanted for us, or what our friends say we're a little crazy for attempting. If we can relax and be in full alignment with ourselves, we see that life feels good. Seated in Self, the sutras say, our "insight is full of order."

"We may lose and we may win," sing the Eagles, and I'd only half agree. But I can fully embrace their insistence that "we will never be here again." If we can't appreciate our stand in life now, then when?

I dial David. He answers on the first ring. "I'll see you in Phoenix on Friday," I say before I can change my mind. "Star's ready to go and so am I!" He sounds genuinely happy, which of course delights me. But it isn't his approval or my guilt or boredom that instigated that call. *Dharma* made me do it.

The call may have been brief but it was a major, could-practically-hear-my-bones-crack adjustment. I returned to relaxing on the couch, and this time I really sunk into it. Into the cushions and my green tea and the company of my dog and to what I was sure was the presence of God, he both subtler and stronger than I expected.

Contentment

Vrksasana
Tree

13

The Sound Of Silence

Mangos are such a big deal on Maui, some people mark their calendars with their seasonal arrival. Our little cottage on the island has an enormous tree of her own. Not just any old mango tree, mind you; she's practically famous island-wide for her luscious fruit. Our backyard explodes with her gifts during the summer months, dropping, during her peak, as many as 40 a day. These lovely mornings, even before coffee, I tiptoe into the backyard to see how many she's given us overnight. I stand there and think that what I love even more than her fruit, if that's humanly possible, is how she has led me to friends and neighbors, some of whom I otherwise would never have met. She's majestic and a connector, and that's her true sweetness, way beyond the fruit she bears.

Around 10pm last night I heard a crash in the backyard—wood splintering followed by a soft landing. I assumed it was our guests returning home after their evening at a luau, entering through the side gate. Without much more thought, I rolled over and went back to sleep.

At sunrise, I rounded the corner and to my dismay, found that one of our tree's major branches had broken clean off. Hundreds of green mangos had fallen to the earth; many hadn't even had the chance to ripen. I looked at her and almost started weeping. This beauty David and I cherished had broken under the weight of her own fruit.

Brokenness is a term replete with spiritual teachings and can carry myriad meanings: messiness, imperfection, the untidiness of being human. I wince at the mere use of the term, even if I use it quite often myself, particularly—or, really, exclusively—in internal conversations. I despise weakness, which, of course, leads to a great deal of suffering since few things in this world are lasting, linear, or predictable.

Mangos themselves don't follow a straight line; they aren't native to Hawaii. They've only been in the islands since the early 19th century, but they are so loved they feel almost indigenous to modern day Hawaiian culture.

Perhaps this is because there's an unsung magic in mangos. Besides their bright, cheery color and delicious taste, they're exceedingly nutritious. They're jam packed with all the best vitamins—A, B, C—and provide fiber, folate, copper, you name it. They make you feel good on the inside, and it shows when they're in season: The aloha spirit—which is a real thing—is even more palpable than usual.

And yet, they're loved as much as they're feared. The coconut wireless tells us stories about mango allergies that have sprung up in this friend's child and that neighbor's wife. You don't even have to eat the mango to suffer from a bad reaction: Their peel can cause a vicious, blistering rash.

"Vicious" and I are bedmates when it comes to mornings with David, even on mornings when I don't wake up to find that the largest branch of the only tree I've ever felt was part of the family sheared off. I wanted to tell him about the tree but, like most mornings, I was hushed with a single raise of his finger to his lips. Sometimes I don't know if he's a mango I should grab or whose skin I shouldn't dare touch, lest I break out in hives.

It's commonly known but easily forgotten that over half of human communication is nonverbal. As a yogi this is fascinating. As a woman living with her husband for weeks on end in a bus with two feet between us, it's excruciating. George Bernard Shaw said, "The single biggest problem in communication is the illusion that it's taking place." Anthony Robbins claims, "The way we communicate with others and with ourselves ultimately determines the quality of our lives." Which, I was convinced, meant my relationship was that very thing I reviled: Weak, and subject to breaking with one wrong turn of the trade winds.

For a man who has made a living from his words, David, in everyday life, speaks very few. I've never considered myself much of a Chatty Cathy, but a "good morning" or "how are you today?" sure would be nice, especially when we're out on tour and I'm out of my element. I'm lucky to hear any words at all before noon.

Marriage can be a lonely affair. No one talks about this, and no one would believe it from my lips, considering that David and I are practically joined at the hip not just for hours on end, but *months*. But his silences are infuriating and they make my insecurities louder. It's isolating to feel unheard. It's also unsatisfying and distressing, especially for needy types like me. *I'll show him*, I think in my infinite maturity. *I'll give him a taste of his own medicine.* I embark on a vow of silence.

But, let's face it, my silence isn't like David's *I'm minding my own business* silence, his *just because I'm up early in the morning doesn't mean I'm a morning person* quietness. Mine is a furious silence, and it's hurled specifically in his direction. It's a *hello, can't you see I need to be acknowledged for the amazing person I am* silence and a *you dragged me all the way out here on tour with you and you can't even look up from your corn flakes?!?!* silence.

My muzzle stays on for all of two hours. It might be still and quiet on the bus or in our Maui kitchen, but we are in conversation, believe me. This is how it usually goes: I'm drinking a fresh fruit power smoothie and glaring at him as he finishes his cereal and moves on to his plate of eggs. I'm disappointed, for no real reason I can actually pinpoint. I just think he should be…different. More excited to greet the day, like I am. More appreciative of me here, right across the counter from him. I think, *something's so wrong with him.* He's just sitting there, quietly enjoying his breakfast, and me? I just can't help myself: I break the silence by launching into him about going to the gym. I hassle him about creating a post for his Facebook fan page. Then I hustle him to call the tree doctor, right now, immediately. I stir the peace right out of the wonderful morning air; I don't even give the day the chance to ripen.

But even more often, my silence causes my fury to ricochet back into my heart, where it beats with a steady insistent tug and lodges there, only adding to this aging process I so often bemoan. After all, it burns a lot of energy to be worried and anxious all the time. This unhealthy rhythm can only be interrupted when I'm aware to conserve what's left of my vitality on any given day, to stop reaching out for happiness, to stop molding others in my perceived image of awesome, and mainly, to quit hating what I have. I'm fixated on fixing him and us, and well, frankly, anything in close enough range, even things that aren't broken. But that mango tree? Well, it *is*.

It doesn't occur to me until I'm in a yoga class the next morning that what's actually broken is this sense of discontent I carry with me like an extra limb. I've come to depend on it, really, because it takes the focus off of myself and out into external circumstances—which I know I have no control over—but what's the harm in trying to fix them, anyway?

Everything, yoga says, just as the class gets quieter and we're led into tree pose. As I've mentioned, one of the translations of yoga is "to yoke," which has come to be defined as union. The practice promotes relationship and intimacy and acceptance—not just with our minds, bodies, and spirits, but also with all of nature and the humans that comprise a large part of it. *The divine in me bows to the divine in you* is the definition of Namaste, which in India is not the tidy end to a yoga class but a salutation, a farewell, a prayer. It makes you curious, if you think about it, that every living thing has a light within them that cannot be broken by rogue winds or grumpy morning behavior. It's curious, too, to consider that my own divine light might shine a little brighter if I could just shut up and Let. Things. Be.

"Silence," my teacher Ravi Ravindra once said, "isn't an absence of sound and stillness isn't an absence of motion. It's a quality of being."

Being is what tree poses demands of us—both this morning on the mat and in all of the tree poses that I've done in my 17 years of practice. It's a common asana, and it was my first standing balance pose. There's a certain contentment to the posture, in that it allows us to see that even when we have only foot on the earth, we are grounded; the pose itself, like my mango tree, is a reminder that *we* are capable of being great connectors. Traditionally in the pose, the hands are held in prayer at the heart. The feet, said to be the motor organ of the will, are asymmetrical and yet the whole heart stays balanced while the hands quietly hold us center at the *anahata*. One translation of which, I should add, is unstruck sound.

Sound is the essence of all vibration. Tesla said, "If you want to know the secrets of the universe, think in terms of energy, frequency, and vibration." The first vibration was "unstruck," meaning it occurred at a time when there were no things to strike against each other to make a peep. That first subtle vibration, the sound behind the sound, is, I believe, the truth behind our thoughts. It's the drop in my stomach when I realize something profound. It's also the ringing in my ears when the saner side of me says, *do you really need to start an argument at 9am just because you need a little attention?*

In tree pose I can see that while there's a degree of mastery in my outermost layer, I can also see I'm holding back, suspicious, really, to give it my all. My toes are unsteady. I tremble, quiver, and grip. It's imperceptible to most, but when I really pay attention, when my mind quiets the incessant chatter of *fix it now, fix it forever, you need to fix, fix, fix,* I find the seed layer that demands, *look at me and love my pose. Love me anyway.*

There's a stuckness there, encased in the memory of slicing it open when I was 10. I was at summer camp, a place on a lake in the Texas hill country I loved so much I went every year for 12 years. Sessions lasted a month, which is a long time to be away from your parents when you're a kid. But Camp Longhorn was magical. It was non-stop fun, and I never missed my mom or dad, that is until that day I landed in the infirmary with toe blood all over my burnt-orange steer-faced t-shirt and got stitched up right then and there on the cold picnic table. Without warning. Without my mom, or my favorite counselor, or my best bunkmate. It stung like hell but I swallowed the pain whole with such determination the lump in my throat ached as much as my filleted foot. I didn't shed a tear. I didn't dare show I was terrified. I stayed silent. And I was rewarded with a merit badge and an *attagirl,* and sent right back out to join my cabinmates in archery class, just in time for target practice.

I never gave my toe much thought until yoga class decades later when I could finally cry; when I could experience the pain of feeling unseen and unheard, of feeling alone against the world, start to release—not just from my toe but from my whole body. This was also the day I began to think of the word contentment not as something grandmothers did or hippies decreed but as something totally essential. The second *niyama*, or inner observances, put forth by Patanjali, claims that contentment speaks to finding peace in the way things are, because the way things are, are correct and ordered, lined up for your soul's target practice perfectly. Contentment resets your emotional compass from harsh and barren conditions to a fluffy, spacious place of *no conditions*.

Emptiness in the Buddhist concept, *sunyata*, is a state encouraged; it's a place devoid of hate or delusion. It's an openness, conducive to liberation. Artist Paul Simon wrote alone in a dark bathroom producing some of the most extraordinary music in rock-and-roll history. *Hello darkness, my old friend*, from his song "The Sound of Silence" reminds us of the value of emptiness—not something to be feared, but something to be embraced.

Simon's song is said to be written in response to angst and the lack of communication between people. *People talking without speaking, People hearing without listening*, he croons, and don't I know it. With 35 concert dates looming ahead, the journey will be impossible to make without communication. If my tree pose could learn to balance from a big toe that doesn't bend, I thought, I could learn to respond to David, or anybody else for that matter, from a place of unwavering contentment.

In theory, anyway.

Because let's be real: A lot of things are bothering me. While spiritual teachings urge detachment from the "fruits of our actions," I'm feeling my fruit hasn't even had time to bud, much less ripen. As I age I see myself waning: my muscles, my tendons, my joints, my verve. I don't have the energy I once did. My mojo to do everything I want to accomplish in a day is fickle and moody, and yet every night I get frantic about how I am going to finish my list with what's left of my life. This is annoying, honestly. Time is taking on a new, more urgent meaning. Purpose is becoming truly important; change, instead of appreciating where I am, feels central. But, like those green mangos that will never make their full journey into the hands of so many mango lovers, nothing is going to really change in my relationship with David, just as his morning quietness isn't likely to alter. Until, of course, I learn to be content with myself, and content—or at least *okay*—with his silences.

Contentment isn't a giving in to mediocrity or giving up on healthier versions of Self, but it does require clarity and an acknowledgement of the here and now. It asks for a willingness, a fiery desire even, to see both the mango tree and the mess of fruit to pick up. All I see is that damn broken branch, and that man who won't talk before lunch. I see my life and my haven't-yet-accomplished-them dreams; and a make-believe calendar that says 58 is too old, too late in the season to start living, really living. There are days when just getting out of bed and walking out to the mango tree feels like a marathon.

But, days after our tree's collapse, the sun casts a warm, golden hue over the whole backyard, and as I shift my view to what's still standing, I contemplate this splendid, massive force of nature. I marvel at her trunk and arms, her malachite green leaves and those oh-so-luscious mangos. She fills me with breath. Literally. Trees metamorphose carbon dioxide and supply oxygen. This invisible miracle strikes me silent and we stand together in the dawn's light, breathing together.

Trees have long been symbolic of the grand inhale and exhale, of life itself. My mango tree broke a limb and isn't worried in the least about fixing it. The tree doctor said she needs special tending to keep her branches pruned back so that her trunk can support her ample abundance. I get that. There are attitudes I'll have to discard if I really want to be content, just as there are things that I need to toss out, like boxes full of 3" high heeled shoes—even the fanciest and most glamorous of them, like my zebra-striped, rhinestone-studded favorites I have counted on for years to make me happy. There was a time when they looked sexy but now, at my age, they look plain silly. I too am changing seasons, along with my mango tree. Maybe it's time to look at brokenness in a new light, for as Twyla Tharp said, "As we grow older, it is just as important to break habits as it is to make them."

Socrates famously said, "Heal thyself." The *Bhavad Gita* says a yogi raises the Self by the Self. At some point you have to ditch "I'm broken" for, as the Tibetans say, "Already Healed, Already Whole." I'm learning to soften my front floating ribs and root down through my tailbone, to give myself literally more breathing room. Tree pose is teaching me how to integrate my own body, not in hiding my weakness but literally by stepping into her.

True magnificence and sturdiness just don't happen out of nowhere, after all; they are seeds that have been planted. Standing below my mango tree's branches—at least those that are left—I'm reminded that even when she's not bearing fruit, she is graceful and effortless and robust in her *tree-ness*. Always lovely to look at, too, and her shade is a welcome reprieve from the hot south Maui sun.

The pose she inspired also calls up relationships. Iyengar said, "How can you know God if you don't know your big toe?" While enunciations by great sages aren't meant to be taken literally—spiritual matters are much more mystical than that—he's making a point that the search for love isn't Out There. It's in our everyday relationships. In my case, however, my big toe actually *did* teach me a lot about God because it gave me a tipping point, literally, in practicing contentment. With a toe that is perfectly imperfect. With a husband who doesn't wish me good morning. With hard conversations with myself about my need to fix everything in sight.

This is ridiculously hard to do *in practice*. But I can catch glimpses of the fruits of my efforts. Like weeks later noticing our tree continues to thrive in spite of losing her branch. While I miss that long brown branch, there is also beauty in her brokenness.

Contentment is becoming intimate, in the words of Paul Simon, "friendly," with the darkness, the brokenness, the noise of our own mental chatter, and becoming deeply committed not to an ideology or a text but to understanding both the world outside us and the movement of our thoughts. The Isa Upanishad says, "From fullness, the fullness is born. Remove the fullness from the fullness and

From fullness, the fullness is born. Remove the fullness from the fullness and fullness alone remains.

✤ *Isa Upanishad*

the fullness alone remains." What's required is acceptance that things can't possibly be other than they are in the present moment. It breaks the myth of the "I'll Be Happy When..." Contentment drops you squarely into the only real existence we can work with—your own life.

We left Maui for our next tour before mango season was over. For me, the unofficial start takes place way before I board our bus. I have to leave Maui first, this place where contentment comes as easy as backyard mangos. The packing is painless because I leave most of my life here. I gather the essentials, some books, my face cream, and my dog, and feel complete. Taking a final look around the house with everything neat and in its place, it's more like an echo chamber of serenity.

This, however, is cut short by David blasting the car horn in the driveway, a wordless and not-so-gentle reminder it's time to leave for the airport. A shiver rolls up my spine as I close our front door, and turn the key until I hear the lock click.

This is the moment where universes collide. The end of Maui Time melts into perpetual forward motion, late nights, close quarters, and noise, noise, noise. But this is also when I can remind myself that I can stay grounded, no matter how quickly the landscape below me is moving.

I narrow my eyes as I glance in the direction of the car horn in an effort to communicate displeasure, but David can't see my eyes underneath my Ray Bans. His elbow is sticking out of the car, resting on the open window. He leans out slightly to catch my glance, and as I bend down to gather my things, he starts to wildly wave his whole arm out the window, twirling his wrists, and pointing his index finger towards the car. He finally speaks, for emphasis, "Come ON already," just in case I didn't get the message.

The world is so impatient.

I exhale deeply, and in the sound of silence that follows, I feel a vision softly creeping. I'm reminded of what God and nature and yoga always tell me: *Your life is not broken. Your relationship is not broken. Nothing is broken because YOU are whole.* They say, *Hear my words that I might teach you*. Learn, I think, instead of repair. A key to stop trying to fix yourself and the world around you is to stop seeing it in disarray, but exactly as it's meant to be.

People pray for contentment all the time, but to make good use of it when it arrives is another story. My next breath is as mighty as my mango tree, and I step forward on my right foot, no longer off balance but perfectly placed atop my right toe. Pressing fully into the meat and using the leverage provided from within, my left foot glides forward smoothly and silently, even elegantly. I stride in the direction of the tour, feeling a newfound stillness. *Now, my dear,* I heard from deep within—the only place where such prudent words can be caught—*You're perfectly aligned. The time is ripe. Now go kick some ass out there.*

As for that horn blowing? That means of communication will be a conversation with my dear husband at another, more fruitful time.

Authenticity

Savasana
Corpse Pose

14

Can't Find My Way Home

In the still of the morning, before my eyes are even open, I'm aware I'm on tour because I hear it: the familiar, buzzy hum of the bus generator. It overpowers those delicate waking voices, those *barely there* whispers that greet you out of a deep sleep. When I went to bed last night I didn't notice any noises at all—in my head or on the bus—probably because, by comparison to a busy show, this home-away-from-home on the Prevost is practically a sanctuary. I tucked in a little after midnight. David was still up, unwinding from the concert by watching a black and white movie on TCM. I, on the other hand, couldn't keep my eyes open. I was in bed before we left the venue parking lot.

Why I rise at 7 in the morning, every morning, even if there is a show the night before, stuns me. The fact is, my body resists the rhythm of life on the road. A not-so-small part of me doesn't cooperate with the nocturnal leanings of a tour schedule. While yoga has taught me to listen to my body—to honor its edges—I spend a lot of time during tour season overriding it, talking my bones down off the ledge. *You can do it! Keep pushing forward. Your 9pm bedtime is for sissies.* After five years of this mental game, I'm still not convinced, not really, and I laugh out loud at this delusion every morning while pondering the great mystery of why I feel slightly south of tired.

I look over at David, who's sleeping so soundly he can't hear my giggle even though I'm close enough to feel his breath. Our little white Maltese, however, is up. She crawls over him and licks his face. He still doesn't budge. Good. Deep sleep is road gold.

It's still dark, inside and out, and I almost step on David's purple-tinted stage glasses haphazardly lazing on the floor. He's always losing them, and I devote part of every day to finding them. Why he can't just put his glasses back in their case and leave them in one place defies reason. But his mind doesn't work in a linear fashion, which makes living with him as hard to predict as the myriad of places where his shades may show up. He's not a man of routine, which is one of the things I admire about him most. He requires me to meet him in the present.

He's so worth it, I say to myself. And I mean every word of it.

This particular morning the generator's steady mechanical whirl doesn't bother me as much as the internal hum of voices that are coming online as I continue to awaken—voices that, through my years of yoga practice, I've come to identify as my parents, my husband, Wall Street, and Madison Avenue (to name just a few). If you ask me, the world's opinions, if left unfiltered, will drown out the beat of your own heart. This noise of unsolicited advice is ubiquitous and hard to tune out no matter how many handstands I do, in skinny jeans, facing backwards, speeding down a highway. But the din is also becoming harder to embrace.

The tour life has been helpful to notice the grooves playing like a record in my mind. I'm amazed these voices show up in Pasadena and Paris, in the snow and in the rain, and on summer mornings, like this one, so full of promise. What's up with these unwelcome visitors telling me I'm not enough? I dress in yesterday's jeans and a fresh t-shirt, run a comb through my hair, and leave in search of coffee, sure a cup of dark roast will wash these voices clean away.

I am always going somewhere or coming back, it seems; relentlessly racing against the clock. I have 28 minutes to make it back on board before we depart. Not 30. Our driver Mr. Grubb is professional and prompt, and his excellence makes me treat our bus call time with the same seriousness.

I pass through a cute urban neighborhood on my walk to the coffee shop I spied the night before on Main Street, a pleasant avenue with flower boxes and manicured lawns. The place is pretty enough to provoke the terminal question, "could I be happy living here?"

The momentum of tour energy is endlessly alluring, largely because it gives me a false sense of outrunning my demons. I convince myself that lasting happiness is right around the next corner; I never cease searching for the place that will make me stop looking. For a person whose lifestyle doesn't even allow me to live in a home most of the year, I devote an enormous amount of energy looking for one. I peruse real estate offices in nearly every city we tour, like a normal person frequents Starbucks. A huge amount of my waking hours on tour are spent on Realtor.com, which provides a quick high for my wound of discontent, a sort of reverse princess-and-the-pea sensitivity that prevents me from finding my kingdom. I feed my underlying discomfort, that *something's not quite right*, by peeking online at houses in Maui, Dallas, Ojai, and the Virgin Islands. If I'm really itchy I'll check out Santa Fe, Paris, Ventura, Miami, and Malibu.

We all know it's not about a house.

In my search for wholeness, for that elusive home within myself, I've blunted myself to my own beauty, desensitized my own feelings, numbed my own superpower of self-love. I've bought into the myth of the white picket fence, and I don't even like that kind of house. The search to "find myself" blinds me from the inherent goodness of my heart, both the easy-to-love aspects and the parts that hold me small and contained in a tidy, easy-to-please shell. The parts that daringly break free when raw authenticity trumps convention.

The lady standing in line in front of me at the coffee shop screams convention. She's beautiful. She's wearing stylish clothes with matching shoes. Her nails are manicured. I lean in closer to confirm my suspicions—she smells like expensive perfume and freshly washed hair. *I bet she's happy as hell,* I say to myself, with a twinge of jealousy. This fast pace has been no defense against deeper feelings. They still come, unbidden.

Apparently I've gotten into her personal space because she turns around to look at me. She's even prettier than previously imagined. "Good morning!" I say with a genuine smile, and as if a miracle descended then and there, I see how good it feels to just be *me*. Me. I bet she spent a full hour to look and smell that good. Me, I've come to delight in my no-makeup-wearing ways, and besides, my feet would ache like crazy in heels that high.

What is it, to find comfort in yourself; to know that your body and bed may change but that the you, the purest side of yourself, will persevere? It's something, alright. It calls to mind Steve Winwood's "Can't Find My Way Home." I don't find it a song of despair or frustration like I used to. Instead, it feels like an anthem of freedom; permission to stop looking. An invitation to inhabit who we are in this very moment. "Somebody holds the key," the song says—and maybe, just maybe, that somebody is me. I'm not saying I haven't had amazing teachers and read countless, helpful books, but it all falls on deaf ears if I don't unlock my own heart, climb in, and do the work. And still. "Do not seek so much you cannot find," Buddha says. At some point you just have to stop and accept yourself, day-old blue jeans, dirty hair and all.

Moving around on tour and in life we take on role after role after role; we define and reinvent ourselves thousands of times. We are all in show business, one way or the other. We all wear masks, only exposing parts of ourselves that are socially acceptable. That will be adored by the crowds.

Yoga, I've come to realize in the most real and lasting of ways, asks us to abandon this behavior and way of thinking. It requires that we live more harmoniously with the calling of our own hearts and not what anybody else says we should do. This takes mad skills. It's also high practice. Unflinching honesty with yourself risks putting your heart on the line for all the world to see; it guarantees a certain degree of heartbreak. But in order to give birth to new, more authentic ways of being, facets of ourselves must die—which may be what St. Paul was thinking when he said "I die daily."

I also die daily, at least on the mat. Savasana encourages us to practice this. It's almost always the last posture, when practitioners are asked to lie down and rest, which is then followed by a reawakening to life. Savasana is a Sanskrit word that combines "corpse" with "seat" or "connection." We invite the experience of death and new life through deep relaxation. It helps us cultivate a state of rest, while also wide awake, by channeling our energy inward. Savasana helps us slow down and receive the subtler, magical wisdom difficult to hear in the usual frantic rhythm of life.

Yogis additionally suggest a practice of pratyahara, which is often translated as a withdrawing of the senses, but in practice it's more of a turning the senses in so that we can hear, taste, smell, touch, and see within, beyond the mind. This is what I love best.

Most people talk about savasana as a moment of peace and quiet, and sometimes it is. But other times, it's chatty, offering wise edits that detangle what's untrue. My most powerful ideas, the ones that have moved my life in bold new directions, have happened in the stillness of savasana, not because they were "my idea" or suggestions from "the voices," but because savasana often delivers out-of-the-blue clarity. Fresh, daring insight. Bigger thinking than either my own benevolent voice or the haunting naysayers could ever come up with. This, I think, is the closest we will ever get to God.

We tirelessly revise and refine ideas about who we are and what our purpose is. "Neti neti," say the yogis, "not this, not that"— referring to our minds, which are too small to ever grasp our magnificence, to fully define the magic. "You wander from room to room looking for the diamond necklace that's already hanging around your neck," Rumi once wrote. How right he was. We will never rest in the pursuit of what we inherently possess. We are, in the end, already home.

"Come down off your throne, and leave your body alone," Winwood sings, which strikes me as a pretty damn concise description of savasana. It requires we clamber out of our ego and become present with what is, no matter what our practice looked like in the preceding minutes. We become aware of our whole self and catch a glimpse of the truth and constancy beneath the noise and movement; of the love beneath the pain.

Where has this led me? How many savasanas have I, really, done? After a lifetime of *should this* and *should that* I've come to the conclusion that you can't be anything other than who you are. This requires no striving or straining or grasping. You are, I believe, enough. Your life, as it is, is your perfect path.

This is the big "so what." There is no storybook ending. There is no levitating, no enlightenment. It's quiet, this realization. It's humbling and stunning, and extraordinarily ordinary.

   This is not to say yoga hasn't changed me. It has, of course. Yogic alignments of how we might engage in our daily lives in a happier, kinder, more easeful manner is in itself a practice, and it is as ongoing and unrelenting and rewarding as sobriety and life and marriage. But spiritual teachings are only maps, and like all maps they point you in the direction but don't get you there. You have to do the work yourself.

   The stylish, impeccable woman returns my morning greeting, and, fortified by two cups of good coffee, I head back to the bus. Even from a block away, my tour-tuned ears can hear that the generator is off and the engine has started, indicating Mr. Grubb is already on board and we're only moments away from wheels-up to the next city. Come to think of it, I have no idea where that might be. I jump up the steps just in time to see Grubb plugging today's coordinates into the GPS.

   "Where to?" I ask.

   "Boise," he says. "Ever been?"

   "Nope."

   "Me either."

   A tacit sense of adventure sets the tone as I pass through to the main cabin of the bus, raise both arms above my head, and enthusiastically relay today's destination to David like it's the most amazing news in the world. He's up now, sitting at the kitchen table-turned-desk. It's not so much to tell him where we're going—surely he already knows—it's more of a greeting, like Good Morning It's Going To Be An Awesome Day And We Get To Go To Boise! He waves me off, though, and puts his forefinger to his lips to shush me as he's on a phone interview with a newspaper in Oklahoma. Undaunted, I settle into my seat at the front of the bus, pretty sure I've had a little too much caffeine.

   Riding up front is my favorite seat in the house, so to speak, with windows so expansive they let the whole world in. With a press of a button on the side of the soft leather chair, the footrest comes out to catch my yoga-and-concert-fatigued legs. The press of another button reclines the back until that perfect spot where it feels like I'm floating in a 3D movie. It's a savasana of sorts, with the grand exception that at this point on our bus trip we've already rolled onto the highway and reached a cruising speed of 65mph. It's anything but still.

Part of me is still in that cute neighborhood, wondering what it would be like to be at home in one of those houses, sipping coffee with my dog on my lap and answering emails. The other part is gliding by. Everything, suddenly, feels fast, too fast. The accumulation of time on the road has reset a rate my body no longer can keep up with. SLOW DOWN, I hear, so loud I look around to see if Grubb or David heard it too. They did not, because insight is a private message. *Just how much of the tour life can a yogi take?* Like all deep secrets wanting to surface, they only do so when one is prepared to listen. I slow myself down with a few deep breaths so as not to shake off the clarity of this message; it feels important not to rush past it.

As if in a parallel universe, David is in the inevitable part of his phone interview where he's being asked when he's going to retire. Even the most seasoned professionals are curious about his superhuman capacity to perform 100 shows annually at the age of 73. I hear him say, "Never." He's always been clear about this. It's not negotiable and I wouldn't want to argue about it with him anyway. When you find someone who is that passionate about his work in the world, I vote to stick close and soak it in. Living with meaning and purpose has irresistible charisma, a surefootedness I admire greatly. David's love of touring and his life as an artist is thick, and somehow works like osmosis. From him, I have learned to love the way of the road.

Or rather, it's him, and myself, that I've learned to love. For real.

Love, I see now, is a practice. All relationships, if they are worth anything, force me to grow, and this road time with David has asked more out of me than I ever thought possible. Not just a change of careers, but a challenge to my whole character. A call to integrity. How we are loving is how we are living and good behavior on weekends every few months doesn't translate to sticking by someone through thick and thin. I could not have imagined the world of rock-and-roll touring would spark such a spiritual journey. I did not know our work together would shake loose my "nice girl" and "dutiful wife" sidekicks, or that in doing so I would be able to see that they were poor trades for self-esteem. I would have never guessed that the greatest temple I would ever pray in would be a cramped tour bus with my husband's purple-tinged sunglasses and handwritten lyrics strewn across floor. You actually have to engage in life and wrestle with strength, gratitude, wonder, contentment, calm, compassion, friendliness, optimism, and trust to give them real meaning. Otherwise it's all just a nice idea.

I wanted love in my life—more than anything—but until I jumped on a tour bus, *his* tour bus, and stuck around a while did I become willing to get a close enough look at what this greatest endeavor of all entails. It's maddening and challenging, even tear-my-hair-out hard, but it's also beautiful in its mundanity and endurance, filled with astonishing moments of grace. It is much like the practice of asana—of yoga itself—where some days on the mat are defined by ease and others contest every bone and muscle and ounce of flexibility I thought I had. But that's the thing: I keep getting on my mat, no matter what. I keep finding David's glasses, no matter what. I keep letting those voices go so that the core of me can be heard over the clamor, also no matter what. All of this—it's what gets me out of bed in the morning, 7am and all. It's the sheer, simple, beautiful joy of this gift I have; that we all have: *I. Am. Alive.* And for this alone, we are, always, home.

"Yoga is the journey of the self through the self to the self," says the *Bhagavad Gita*. So is this rock-and-roll tour life, with David by my side. And what have I found there? That love—all love—is an inexhaustible resource.

Namaste.

We

are all just

walking each

other home.

〰 *Ram Dass*

Endnotes

Chapter 1
Feelin' Alright

Feelin' Alright? was written by Dave Mason and released in 1968.

"True yoga is not about the shape of your body, but the shape of your life. Yoga is not to be performed; yoga is to be lived." - Aadil Palvhival, Fire of Love

"Do you not know that your bodies are temples of the Holy Spirit?" - 1 Corinthians 6:19

"To really become free inside take either courage or disaster." - Christopher Reeve as quoted by Cal Fussmann, Esquire Magazine, January 29, 2007. Esquire.com

"Yoga is breaking the bonds of suffering." - Bhagavad Gita 6:23

In Buddhism, the four noble truths are: Life is suffering. The cause of suffering is craving. The cessation of suffering come with a cessation of craving. There is a path that leads from suffering.

"Here, now, is the teaching of yoga." - Yoga Sutra 1.1, translated by Ravi Ravindra

"It is not the mountains but ourselves that we conquer." - Attributed to Sir Edmumd Hillary in That's Life, Wild Wit & Wisdom (2003) by Bonne Louise Kuchler, p. 20.

"A yogini is a professional of the interior landscape, and expert conservationist of the vital life force, prana." - Tenzin Palmo, Cave in the Snow

"If you see what is, what is changes." - Jiddu Krishnamurti as heard quoted by Ravi Ravindra in a lecture in Ojai, California

The Shiva Purana lists 1008 names for Lord Shiva.

"When negative thoughts or feelings arise, the opposite should be cultivated." - Yoga Sutra 2.33, translated by Ravi Ravindra

Chapter 2
Dream On

Dream On was written by Steven Tyler and released in 1973.

There are many translations of yoga, "Yuj" is one of them.

"There is no value in life except what you choose to place upon it and no happiness in any place except what you bring to it yourself." - Henry David Thoreau. Walden.org says this is a misattribution to Thoreau, citing it belongs to Lin Yulang in his book, On the Wisdom of America (New York: John Day, 1950,) p. 46.

"Because true belonging only happens when we present our authentic, imperfect selves to the world, our sense of belonging can never be greater than our level of self-acceptance." - Brene Brown, Daring Greatly: How the Courage to Be Vulnerable Transforms the Way We Live, Love, Parent, and Lead

"Vulnerability is the birthplace of innovation, creativity, and change." - Brene Brown, TedTalk 2012

"The strongest love is the love that demonstrates its fragility." - Paul Coelho, Eleven Minutes

"The wise man lets go of all results, whether good or bad, and is focused on the action alone. Yoga is skill in action." - Bhagavad Gita, 2:50

Chapter 3
Love The One You're With

Love The One You're With was written by Steven Stills and released in 1970.

"The world is in bondage to work unless they are performed for the sake of yajna (sacrifice). Therefore, O Son of Kunti, give up attachment and do your work as a sacrifice." - Bhagavad Gita 3.4

"Wherever You Go, There You Are: Mindfulness in Everyday Life" by Jon Kabat Zinn was first published in 1994.

The five niyamas are saucha, santosha, tapas, swadyaya, and ishvara pranidad. - Yoga Sutra 2.32

"Your task is not to seek for love, but merely to seek and find all the barriers within yourself that you have built against it." - Rumi

"I would venture to warn against too great an intimacy with artists as it is very seductive and a little dangerous." - Queen Victoria

"To live is to suffer, to survive is to find some meaning in the suffering." - Friedrich Neitzsche

"We are most alive when we are in love." - John Updike

"Love creates a home wherever it is. Love is never in want. True love is always in a state of found." - Hafiz

"Let the beauty we love, be what we do. There are a hundred ways to kneel and kiss the ground." - Rumi, translated by Coleman Barks

"The objective of cleaning is not just to clean, but to feel happiness living within that environment." - Marie Kondo

"Also through cleanliness and purity of body and mind comes a purification of the subtle mental essence, a pleasantness, goodness and gladness of feeling, a one-pointedness with intentness, the conquest or mastery over the senses, and a fitness, qualification, or capability for self-realization." - Yoga Sutra 2.41, Swamij.com

The five kleshas are avidya, asmita, raga, dvesha, and abhinevesha. - Yoga Sutra 2.3

"Not all of us can do great things. But we can do small things with great love." Mother Teresa

"The most important aspect of love is not in giving or the receiving, it's in the being. When I need love from others, or need to give love to others, I'm caught in an unstable situation. Being in love, rather than giving or taking love, is the only thing that provides stability. Being in love means seeing the Beloved all around me." - Ram Dass, RamDass.org

Chapter 4
Shine On You Crazy Diamond

Shine On You Crazy Diamond was written by David Gilmour and released in 1975.

"Continuous care and attention for a long time establishes this practice (abhyasa)." - Yoga Sutra 1.14, translated by Ravi Ravindra

"The success of yoga does not lie in the ability to perform postures but in how it positively changes the way we live our life and our relationships." - T.K.V. Desikachar

The eight limbs of yoga are yama, niyama, asana, pranayama, pratyahara, dharana, dhyana, and samadhi. - Yoga Sutra 2.29

"Yoga isn't about understanding the truth, it's about withstanding the truth." as heard quoted by Ravi Ravindra in a lecture in Ojai, California, at Krotona

"Right alignment is accompanied by steadiness and ease." - Yoga Sutra 2.46, translated by Ravi Ravindra

"Our deepest fear is not that we are inadequate. Our deepest fear is that we are powerful beyond measure. It is our light, not our darkness that most frightens us." - Marianne Williamson, A Return to Love

"Yagnavalkya said, 'Oh Gargi, do not ask too much, lest thy head should fall off. Thou askest too much about a deity about which we are not to ask too much. Do not ask too much, O Gargi.' After that Gargi held her peace." - Brihadaranyaka Upanishad, Part 2, Sixth Brahmana

"Be patient toward all that is unsolved in your heart and try to love the questions themselves like locked rooms and like books that are written in a very foreign tongue." - Ranier Maria Rilke, Letters to a Young Poet

Chapter 5
Landslide

Landslide was written by Stevie Nicks and released in 1975.

"Timeless insight and integration may be reached by self-surrender to God (Ishvara)." - Yoga Sutra 1.23, translated by Ravi Ravindra

"Happiness is the very nature of the self: happiness and the self are no different." - Ramana Maharishi

Chapter 6
Don't Stop Believin'

Don't Stop Believin' was written by Jonathan Cain, Steve Perry, and Neal Schon and released in 1981.

"Bidden or not bidden, God is present" - Desiderius Erasmus, 16th century monk

The myth of Hanuman is found in the Ramayana.

"When the bird and the book disagree, always believe the bird." - John James Audubon

"Faith is not a belief. Faith is what is left when your beliefs have all been blown to hell. Faith is in the heart, while beliefs are in the head." - Ram Dass, Be Love Now: The Path of the Heart

The Buddhist Wheel of Life revolves through six realms, one of which is that of the Hungry Ghost. Dr. Gabor Mate likened this realm to that of addiction.

"The most important decision we make is whether we believe we live in a friendly or hostile universe." - Albert Einstein

Chapter 7
While My Guitar Gently Weeps

While My Guitar Gently Weeps was written by George Harrison and released in 1968.

Karuna is one of Buddhism's four immeasurables.

The word "weep" appears twice in the I Ching: hexagram 3 and hexagram 61.

"If you want others to be happy, practice compassion. If you want to be happy, practice compassion." - Dalai Lama

"The gap between compassion and surrender is love's darkest, deepest region." - Orham Pamuk, The Museum of Innocence

Chapter 8
School's Out

School's Out was written by Alice Cooper, Michael Bruce, Glen Buxton, Dennis Dunaway, and Neal Smith and released in 1967.

"I don't believe in God, but I miss him." - Julian Barnes, Nothing to be Frightened Of

"Let's stop reading about God—we will never understand him." - Hafiz, If It Is Not Too Dark

"Wonder is the foundation of yoga." - Shiva Sutras 1.12

Chapter 9
Tupelo Honey

Tupelo Honey was written by Van Morrison and released in 1972.

The kleshas are listed in Yoga Sutra 2.3.

"Be kind whenever possible. It is always possible." - Dalai Lama

"Yoga doesn't care about where you have been; yoga cares about the person you're becoming." - Aadil Palkhivala, The Fire Of Love

Chapter 10
Sunshine Of Your Love

Sunshine Of Your Love was written by Jack Bruce, Pete Brown, and Eric Clapton and released in 1967.

"It's the lack of love that makes everything stale, dull, and uninteresting." - Ravi Ravindra, The Spiritual Roots of Yoga

The House Divided Speech was delivered by Abraham Lincoln on June 16, 1858, in Springfield, Illinois.

108 is a sacred number in Buddhism and Hinduism.

"Gratitude unlocks the fullness of life. It turns what we have into enough, and more. It turns denial into acceptance, chaos to order, confusion to clarity." - Melody Beattie

"Keep your face always toward the sunshine and the shadows will fall behind you." - Walt Whitman

Chapter 11
Listen To The Music

Listen To The Music was written by Tom Johnston and released in 1972.

"Yoga is establishing the mind in stillness. Then the Seer dwells in its essential nature. Otherwise the movements of the mind are regarded as the Seer." - Yoga Sutras 1.2-1.4, translated by Ravi Ravindra

"Asmita is the misidentification of the power of seeing with what is seen." - Yoga Sutra 2.6, translated by Ravi Ravindra

"Your playing small does not serve the world. There is nothing enlightened about shrinking so that other people won't feel insecure around you." - Marianne Williamson, A Return to Love

"When we feel love and kindness toward others, it not only makes others feel loved and cared for, but it helps us also to develop inner happiness and peace." - Dalai Lama

"The best way to find yourself is to lose yourself in the service of others." - Mahatma Gandhi

"In this body are all the Gods and all the Demons." - Buddha

"Heaven and hell are within us, and all the gods are within us." - Joseph Campbell, The Power of Myth

"Your own self-realization is the greatest service you can render the world." - Ramana Maharishi

Chapter 12
Take It Easy

Take It Easy was written by Jackson Browne and Glenn Frye and released in 1972.

The four aims of life are dharma, artha, kama, and moksha. They are also known as purusharthas and are found in the vedic texts of the Ramayana and the Mahabharata. "Right alignment is accompanied by steadiness and ease." - Yoga Sutra 2.46, translated by Ravi Ravindra

"Our heart is restless until it rests in you." - St. Augustine

"The final obstacle in meditation is ecstasy; you feel great bliss and happiness and want to stay in that ecstasy. Do not yield to it but pass on to the next stage which is great calm. The calm is higher than ecstasy..." - Ramana Maharishi

Chapter 13
The Sound Of Silence

The Sound Of Silence was written by Paul Simon and released in 1965.

"The single biggest problem in communication is the illusion that it has taken place." - George Bernard Shaw

"The way we communicate with others and ourselves ultimately determines our quality of life." - Anthony Robbins

"If you want to know the secrets of the universe, think in terms of energy, frequency, and vibration." - Nikola Tesla

"Happiness can only exist in acceptance." - George Orwell

"Physician, heal thyself." - Socrates

Chapter 14
Can't Find My Way Home

Can't Find My Way Home was written by Steve Winwood and released in 1969.

"I die daily." - St. Paul, 1 Corinthians 15.31

"Pratyahara is the withdrawal of the senses from their objects by following the essential nature of the mind." - Yoga Sutra 2.54, translated by Ravi Ravindra

"You wander from room to room hunting for the diamond necklace that is already around your neck!" - Rumi

Endorsements

"Reading Winifred Wilson's book makes you feel like you've just eaten a great bowl of chicken soup! The way she brings you into her life and tries to help others find peace is beautiful and effective. Some never find the door to start the journey to compassion but she might help you find the key. For anyone searching for joy in this wild and confusing world, *Downdog for Roaddogs* can help you. It's the quiet pond in the middle of a storm."
  - Talent manager, film agent, and producer, "Supermensch" Shep Gordon

"Dear Readers!!! You must have this fantastic magical book, full of pages that are upon every turn, opened up to new insightful ways into ... "God knows." For me, having literally spent my life on the road, this read has taken some broken memories of those years and has, in some instances, turned those memories upside down and into moments of, after this read, magical life lessons that I now hold close to my heart!! Winifred I love you and love this book. It is your song that will stand the test of time!!
  - Musician, actor, co-founder of Fleetwood Mac, Mick Fleetwood

"Winifred Wilson's *Downdog for Roaddogs: Yoga for Rock-and-Roll Tours and Other Cosmic Journeys of the Heart* is a delight to read—and very insightful. Reading this book one can experience how each of the yoga postures can be practiced not only physically but also spiritually, in any place and at any time, leading to life-changing experiences. I would be surprised if this book did not enchant everyone interested in any aspect of yoga."
  - International teacher and author of *The Wisdom of Patanjali's Yoga Sutras*, Ravi Ravindra

"*Downdog for Roaddogs* is a true story of a yogi's life on the rock-and-roll road she shares with husband, long time musician, Dave Mason. I first met Winifred ten years ago and was impressed by the great vision she had for teaching and sharing the benefits of a yoga led life with as many people as possible. I was particularly impressed by Winifred's soulful kindness and her desire to help bring yoga to those in the addiction recovery community to help heal and nourish their bodies and soul. I encouraged her to do it, agreeing that this community would benefit greatly by her vision. Yoga Blue, a yoga program for recovery was the result, and Winifred's dream became a gift for many seeking a new way of living.

In this book, she describes integrating and sharing yoga and the principals of peace and harmony with another type of warrior: the road warrior. While dealing with the insane life backstage and on the tour bus she called home, she describes finding her true self through yoga, love, life, the people she met along the way—and the power of music. Finding this balance is a key to a healthy life. Winifred gives positive direction and advice to help to heal the heart and soul..."

- Two-time Grammy Award-winning singer, songwriter, and social activist, Michael Bolton

"A yogi's quest for self-discovery and equanimity. *Downdogs for Roaddogs* is a love story that shines."

- New York Times Bestselling Author, *Still Alice, Every Note Played, Left Neglected, Love Anthony,* and *Inside the O'Briens,* Lisa Genova, Ph.D

"Winifred and I are fellow Road Dogs. Cut from the same bolt, we are not unlike puppies, who, when car keys are jingled, start to leap around the room in anticipation of going in the car! We both can say we live on a bus, sleep in a bed that moves, and (sometimes) share a toilet with six men. This can be at times...daunting. In her book Winifred manages to capture the thrill of a rock and roll tour, the excitement of being onstage, and the challenges of day to day living out of a suitcase. Her catharsis and transformation through

movement and yoga make *Downdog for Roaddogs* an eye-opening and compelling read."
  - Dancer, award-winning choreographer, co-founder of Solid Rock Teen Center, and wife of Alice Cooper, Sheryl Cooper

"Winifred Wilson is the real deal. Many of us study the yogic principles, but Winifred embodies them. *Downdog for Roaddogs* take us through humorous, yet heartbreaking explorations of real-life relatable scenarios. The wisdom Winifred shares transforms ancient yoga concepts into practical guideposts for people living in the modern world.

Her stories are compelling, funny and engaging to the point that you almost forget that you're learning yoga—until suddenly you are hit with the truth. Winifred presents lessons steeped in wisdom that only lived experience and inner sight can produce. Like a master weaver, she pulls on the threads of asana, philosophy, the poetry of song, and the vulnerable grit of life to create a beautiful text that both entertains and educates.

Downdog for Roaddogs is wildly entertaining, but it is also an important yogic text—one that reminds us that yoga is ultimately a practice of relationship, clear vision, truth, and love."
  - Author of *Follow the Feeling: A Roadmap to Emotional Freedom*, Lisa West

"Incredible…life on the road is not as easy and glamorous as it looks, but if there's one person who makes it look effortless, it's Winifred Wilson."
  - Co-founder of *Harley Women*, author of *The American Motorcycle Girls*, and wife of The Doobie Brothers' Pat Simmons, Cris Sommer Simmons

"Not surprised Winifred has written a revolutionary book about yoga as a way of life no matter what your life is in this present moment. This will become a dog-eared book for many on the road of life."
  - Founder of Desk Yogi and Punk Wellness, Jacqui Burge

How we are

loving

is how we are

living.

-Winifred Wilson

The Author

Winifred Wilson is a yoga teacher and music executive who splits her time between South Maui, Northern Nevada, and a rock-and-roll tour bus. Raised in Dallas, Texas, she studied in Honolulu, Paris, Austin, and New York City before completing her MBA at Pepperdine University. After attending Sotheby's American Arts Program, she went on to hold a 20-year career in the retail fine art industry, ultimately running six galleries in three states.

In 2009, Winifred founded Yoga Blue, a nonprofit dedicated to teaching yoga to those recovering from substance abuse and other self-destructive behaviors. Endorsed by two-time Grammy Award winner Michael Bolton, the outreach organization provided classes to at-risk and under-served populations in California's Ventura and Santa Barbara counties. Winifred has also served on the board of several establishments, including the Nevada Women's Fund and the Sierra Arts Foundation.

Winifred has been on the road with her husband—one of the founding members of Traffic and Rock-and-Roll Hall-of-Famer Dave Mason—since 2010, supporting Mason and his band at over 100 shows annually. She teaches yoga and journaling workshops at various stops around the country, blogs regularly at winifredwilson.com, and has served on the staff of Ojai's Lulu Bandha's, Reno's Yoga Loka, the Wailea Yoga & Dance Shala, Kihei's 808 Wellness, and Maui Yoga Path. *Downdog for Roaddogs* is her first book.

Colophon

This book is the fruit of a life dedicated
to traveling the way of the heart.

The first edition is a print run of 750.
It is printed by offset lithography on
Mohawk Via 80# Text Smooth Pure White and bound
by Roswell Bookbinding in Phoenix, Arizona.

The design is by Norman Clayton in Ojai, California.
The book is typeset in Weiss designed by Emil Rudolf Weiss.

With gratitude...